T0194201

ALVIN WALLACE

Relationships

Love, Sex, and Marriage

iUniverse, Inc.
Bloomington

Relationships
Love, Sex, and Marriage

Copyright © 2011 Alvin Wallace

iUniverse books may be ordered through booksellers or by contacting:

iUniverse
1663 Liberty Drive
Bloomington, IN 47403
www.iuniverse.com
1-800-Authors (1-800-288-4677)

ISBN: 978-1-4502-9092-0 (pbk)
ISBN: 978-1-4502-9093-7 (ebk)

Printed in the United States of America

iUniverse rev. date: 2/1/2011

Love is mentally powerful and physical and can be psychologically destructive, and blind. There are many definitions and expressions of what love is. But when you violates that trust, that unity, and that relationship between each other it becomes a hatred force of destruction and dangerous of being destroy due to the forth of nature within as our feelings begins to turn cold seeking out vengeance of satisfaction, as our heart begins to heal the painfulness of sorrow while pulling the spear from within slowly to avoid tearing the tenderness of love that might had been left behind.

What this mean?"Love is as strong as hate". Love is like making a promise between "two people". Its like saying "I do" but without the words. Love is nothing to play with. The love between two people are special. Its nothing like nothing else in this world. You can't measure it, you can't shake it with a stick, you can't point a figure at it, and its damn hard to get back when its gone.

Everyone have their own definition of love. What is love to you? Some say love is just having respect for each other. There is no right or wrong answers. If that is love where does it begin? Only you can say what love is. Because is its different to everyone. Love is how you treat yourself and others. Love is how you choose to be treated.

"Action speaks louder than words". There are times when the treatment of love or the lack of it is forced on you, and literally tearing your gusts out. Its enough to make you scream and cry for mercy. There are no bounds. No one in a relationship especially when your married appreciate being cheated on by their spouse with others. Having if you will sexually intercourse in the person's house. Its just a question of "how low can you go". First of all if you love your spouse, man or woman, why would you allow yourself to undertake such a thing of betrayal destroying such a beautiful loving relationship? That is beyond me. So, I asked you again, what is love? Surely this is not. This is more like a derailed train heading for the gates of hell. There is a strange thing about love. Is there a relationship without love? Your actions, respond to feelings, and emotions of the other person will determine the answer to those questions.

If that's true why do people do things knowing that it will hurt the other person? let me say this. Sometime a person will do things without first thinking about the pain that follow, and the effect it will have on that person.

We sometime speaks out of tongue, and despite everything we have a tendency to say the wrong things. A person will sometime do things just to do spark a reaction. A person will do things complaining and using sex as an excuse, sex not pleasing, not satisfying, and not fulfilling. It could be a sign and a message telling you that he /she don't love you anymore.

But if that's true why don't the person get a divorce or file for a temporary separation? Why stay there and suffer, why stay together at all, and what have they to gain?"Your damn if you do and your damn if you don't". Their headed down the road of destruction. Its only time when shit is going to hit the fan. Then your going to say, "Oh" my God what am I going to do now?"Its too late". Its like waiting for a volcanic to erupt. If that person is sick should that person remain in the relationship? Or is it all about money?

Women have been known to leave men who are sick and disabled. Why? First of all financially, and secondly they cannot, cannot satisfy them sexually in bed."That's a blow". A blow but true. I remember a man a few years ago telling me that his wife left him for that very same reason. I'm very serious."Don't ever take your relationship for granted. Tomorrow, it could be over. Whatever happened to marriage vows, promises, and I do? That wasn't important anymore! It does make you wonder if that person was seeking someone else long before that, and therefore used it as an excuse or a stepping stone if you will to leave. Are you telling me that marriage is all about money?

What about love? What about the relationship? Have you heard this expression?"You cannot live on love alone"? Ask yourself does that make sense? But relationships do remain as such despite their differences. But the love slowly dies and eventually crumbles."Be that as it may". Life must go on. Why push the button of destruction? Whatever happened to "For better or for worse"? No one wants the worse. A relationship was meant to grow and become better and better. Who wants worse? People get into a relationship especially marriages for "better". Lets stop here for a second.

What does the dictionary say about love, relationships, and marriage? Love, and I quote, strong affection for another arising out of kinship or personal ties—attraction base on sexual desires, affection and tenderness felt by lovers. Affection based on admiration and benevolence or common interests, warm attachment, enthusiasm, or devotion.

Love, according to Frank Vilaasa, and I quote, is the energy that connects us to other people and to life itself. Love is nourishment for the heart and soul. Without it we feel our separation from others as painful and lonely. We may live a life of physical comfort, with lots of activity to stimulate the body and mind, yet we will still feel acutely that something is missing. We may attempt to dull it through work. Food, sex, alcohol, entertainment, etc. yet in our most honest moments we know that we are just trying to distract ourselves, and that none of these things will satisfy our deepest need. He said the quest for love starts when we admit this need to ourselves, and make a decision to do whatever is necessary to find the love we long for, unquote. Well, as you can see the depth of the story expresses a lot concerning relationships and other things of importance as human beings and as people in relationships experiences everyday of their lives.

The problem is how do we deal with it and how does it affects the other person? Speaking of that lets take a look at an article by Lawrence Mitchell, and I quote, Fighting With Your Woman The Right Way, Because I consider myself a relationship advocate he said for men everywhere. It is with shame that I make a most painful admission.

Men he said are inferior when it comes to conflict resolution. We are. Admit it. Whether in an argument, a mild disagreement or a fight, we need a lesson on how to make it work with our significant other. The problem with us he said, as men, is that we see life in terms of competition

We process he said in such a rational, logical fashion that we tend to alienate our partner. Sure, we make our point and may even "win" the argument. But what do we gain in the long run? Again, our competitive institution is a hindrance when we disagree with a woman.

Take a break to clear your head, in the event that the argument is severe and about to explode, leave. Walk away and cool your head. Contain the eruption because in the end, both of you may regret what was said and done. Once you let the quarrel degenerate into personal attacks and even physical confrontation, you can never go back and erase the harm. I can never forget the first time my first love he said and I swore at each other. I he said had made a promise never to use profanity toward her but in a moment of weakness, I gave in to temptation. And so did she. The result he said was a sweet innocence lost and a dangerous precedent set. Do not he said let the same thing befall your relationship. Go to bed on common ground, I he said advocate you clear your heads but at the same time, try to nip the problem in the butt as soon as possible."Never go to bed mad" is a common axiom for couples.

I do not agree for the pure fact that it is not realistic advice. What are you to do? Stay up all night? My spin is to never go to bed without some sort of agreement in place. Even if you are upset he said at her and vice versa, at a minimum agree to get together the next day to discuss the problem in a civil manner. If you live together, however, that advice may not fly.

Rather than sleep on the couch, I urge you to live that extra effort to resolve the conflict. If you hit a dead end, agree to sleep on it until the next day. The bottom line for us as men he said is to realize that we usually fight in a different manner than women. But our logical, competitive nature cannot dominate our relationship conflicts. We lose out in the end that way.

Therefore he said, we have to make it our mission not to cower or repress our outrage, but to remain open, respectful, compassionate, and communicative. And remember that overall, indifference and not anger or wrath is the real enemy in a relationship. Address the current fight, Simple advice he said, but for many, a major roadblock to conflict resolution.

The ride is smooth he said (as smooth as a fight can be), the end is in sight, then all of a sudden, wham! you remind your girlfriend about why she was wrong the last time there was a major argument. Bad move slick. Never, ever, rehash the past. Leave it there and focus on the fight at hand. Disagree, rant and rave all you want. Just be sure to make it all about the current problem and not that she left for dead a year ago. Avoid the blame game, Again, as a men, it may feel good to win the battle and come out on top. But appearances can be deceptive.

What you conclude as a victory is a complete loss in the long run, when you factor in her resentment toward you and the lack of goodwill on her part. If you push her to admit she was wrong, apologize and break down in tears, what do you suppose that will do to her in the long—term love for you? Not a pretty picture is it?

Take your finger out of her face and remember, this is your women. Love her even when the going is rough. She is not the enemy. Discuss and fight like an adult, Contrary to popular opinion, a fight need not be a verbal brawl. It can fall into the domain of courteous debate and expression.

Not to say that you have to scream every word and to fake, but at the same time, keep that temper in check. Lower your voice and avoid the exaggerated body language. Never, ever be aggressive toward your lady love in a physical way. Be a gentleman and have some respect, not just for her, but also for yourself. One tip! I recommend is to approach he said an argument as if a camera is on the two of you.

Try to be warm, Let me expand on the point that you have to fight on a foundation and premise of love. By that I mean he said that even if you are in a rage at a wrong she committed, it is beneficial to remember just who she is. She is the love of your life. Implicit in that role is a dose of respect when a disagreement is about to flare. You must communicate he said with her in a manner unlike anyone else. Maintain eye contact and even touch her arm or hand when appropriate. No matter who is upset at whom he said, let her know that underneath it all, you love and will forgive, or if you are the cause, feel repentant, unquote. Why men and women argue differently, by Damian Whitworth, and I quote, In Gapun, a emote village on the Sepik River in Papua New Guinea, the women take a robust approach to arguing.

In her pithy new book The Myth of Mars and Venus, Deborah Cameron reports an anthropologist's account of a dispute between a husband and wife that ensued after the woman fell through a hole in the rotten floor of their home and she blame him for shoddy workmanship.

He hit her with a piece of sugar cane, an unwise move that led her to threaten to slice him up with a machete and burn the home to the ground. At this point Damian Whitworth said he deemed it prudent to leave and she launched into a kros-a traditional angry tirade directed at a husband with the intention of it being heard by everyone in the village.

The fury can last for up to 45 minutes, during which time the husband is expected to keep quiet. This particular kros went along these lines:"You're a rubbish man. You hear? Your prick is full of maggots. You have built me a good house that I just fall down in, you get up and hit me on the arm with a piece of sugar cane!

You! Mother's! Human beings argue about everything from adultery to Zionism and we do so in different styles, whether we are submissive, passive, aggressive, abusive, abusive-passive, aggressive-abusive, submissive-passive. Tim Smith is a psychology professor at the University of Utah, whose own research has found indications that women's heart health is affected adversely by quarrels and men's when they feel they are losing control.

He says that it is a male tactic to withdraw from arguments. Women he said on average are more often in the role of the managers of relationship matters. They are often in the position of bringing up and pursuing things they would like to change. This is seen in wives making a request and pursuing it and husbands withdrawing and pulling back. Gary's thesis is that the differences and disagreements between men and women don't hurt so much as the ways in which we communicate them. Feeling challenged, the man becomes focused on being right and forgets to be loving.

The woman then becomes upset by his unloving delivery and defends herself from his sharpened expressions. Her tone becomes mistrusting and rejecting. Most arguments he said escalate when a man begins to invalidate a woman's feelings and she responds to him disapprovingly."But Northam adds that in her experience of many years of helping couples, the way men and women have been conditioned affects the way that they argue and that it true that men have a greater tendency to withdraw.

One popular phrase among psychologist she said, is" the distancer and the pursuer", says Northam." One of you wants to sort it and the other one backs off: I will shut down and I won't deal with you. That does lead to a lot of tension in the relationship and you end up not addressing what you need to be talking about.

I do talk with men who find it very, very difficult to engage with their feelings. Women she says: He won't respond to me, he won't listen he thinks he's right all the time. Men have been socialistic to think that they know what they are talking about.

I know it's changing; it's really changing a lot. But that's still around: Men are powerful and what I say goes. Women intermalise that too. It's not just the blokes. Women get very frustrated, hysterical, when trying to get their point across because it seems that it just falls on the dead ground all the time. What they are saying is not being picked up and acknowledged and dealt with. Certainly the younger men that I see tend to be much more willing to engage with their feelings, keen to understand them and talk about them.

Older men find it slightly trickier or more than slightly trickier". She adds that women are also capable of the withdrawal technique."Oh yes, women are quite powerful at doing that as well. They change the subject or rubbish it or cry.

Christine Northam says that another major differences between the way men and women argue is that" men tend to resort to aggression very quickly, whereas women are manipulative and try and present a problem and go on and on about it rather then being succinct.

Men get angry and feel defensive and shameful very quickly, then they get aggressive. She says that men are also more prone to decline to take their partner's concerns seriously."They say: She's going on again. Oh, here we go. They tend to trivialize. I'm afraid it goes back to our pattering; the stereotypical stuff we have all been fed.

We are very much influenced by the way our parents were or even our grandparents. We all like to think we are terribly different but we are not, unquote. Lets talking about Body Language in Intimate Relationships. According to an article from the internet and I quote, The issue of body language within intimate relationships is quite complex and one that is not easily broken down into specific, predictable definitions. It is much like a dance between two people, constantly in motion and combining with other aspects of the relationship to communicate a wide variety of messages.

Eye contact and I quote, is important because it indicates interest; body position is also important because it helps to indicates comfort levels. As the relationship progresses, more and more touching occurs. This shows up as holding hands, hugging, learning each other, and the like. When two people in an established intimate relationship use body language, it can take on far more subtle meanings. This is especially true if the relationship is troubled in some way or if there is verbal communication between them.

It is quite common for couples to use body language when they are unwilling or unable to talk about a conflict openly. Either person might withdraw physically or emotionally from the other avoiding the situations of physical closeness and keeping feelings inside. Or, either person might become quite physical by slamming the door banging drawers shut, vigorously cleaning something, or the like. When it comes to communicating intimacy, and I quote, though, body language is perhaps the most powerful tool available to couples. A touch of the hand, an arm around the shoulder. a tender kiss on the cheek. or a tender caress of the cheek are all great examples of ways couples expresses intimacy with each other. In general, body language in intimate relationships serves a vital purpose. It communicates specific type of information when a relationship is relatively young as well as when it is more established, quoted.

Marriage, and I quote, The state of being married. The mutual relationship between husband and wife. The institution whereby men and women are jointed in a special, and of social and legal dependence for the purpose of founding and maintaining a family.

Relationship, and I quote, The state of character of being related or interrecord. State of affairs existing between those having relations or dealing with his family, unquote. Jusus Nawrae, and I quote, Play of natture: a sport or freak of nature. Passion, and I quote, full of vitality, full of strength. Lust, and I quote, to have an intense desire or need, to have a sexual urge.

Sex, according to Walter Mosley, and I quote, is everything from the bananas and figs we eat to guns and lips of the tongue. Sex governs he said most of our relations and all of our creative activities. And so it is no surprise that sex is one of the main metaphors in understanding our actions. For instant he said, I was once asked by a woman who wanted to be a writer, how I found the discipline to write everyday. My response to her was simple. If you had a friend who told you that every morning when she awake up the first thing she did was to make love to her husband," I asked," would you ask her how she found the discipline to do such a thing?" The laughed. Who needs discipline to make love"

All you need is the passion and blood and everything else is easy. Sex comes naturally, as do all things we love.

But he said there's another aspect to sex and writing!. it is also very, very particular. As a writer he said I have learned anytime you write about sex in such a way it merely arouses the reader, you have failed to capture the ambivalence and the desperation involved whenever two or more human beings truly come together. Sex doesn't always happen between lovers. Sometime a seemingly willing partner is unwilling on the inside.

Sometime sex is revenge or payment or just a good way to work off tension so you can get to sleep. Sex doesn't smell like roses. It's not hairless, breathless, or necessarily beautiful. Sex is rife with bodily odors and violent gestures. Lovers scream and curse and do things that are not always acceptable to others. Sex that drives us away as well as pulls us in is the best sex there is, unquote.

Here's what great sex isn't, according to Brian Velenchenko, and I quote, gadgets, bedroom tips, tiny blue pills, or girl gone wild. At heart it's a primal form of comfort, a kind of conversation, the ultimate, most gloriously soul-baring dissolver of boundaries. This month's O takes sex seriously, from the truth about women and casual encounters to advice from the sexperts to the body, rattling revelations of some very candid writers, unquote.

14 Really good sex questions by Carol Mithers, and I quote, Can you learn to be passionate about someone if there's no chemistry at first, If a couple like each other, have fun together, and basically have a good relationship, they shouldn't call it quits if everything is there but the sex. Chemistry can grow if you give yourself permission to learn about yourself as a sexual human being and to communicate your desires. Can you have a great, long lasting sex life with the same partner? Absolutely, but you're not going to be having movie style sex.

Movie sex is romantic and passionate: You idealize your partner; you're turned on even before you begin, and you make love every time you're together. In an ongoing relationship, sex is more about intimacy and security, and it's integrated with who you really are.

It also doesn't happen as often. Couples who keep their sex lives going develop a style early on, who initiates, how much foreplay is included, do they like taking turns, do they or don't they appreciate quickies. They also consciously make time for sex. The more you avoid having sex and the more self conscious you become about it, the harder it is to get back on track.

What is the latest on sex toys? So many people are using them. Vibrators have helped some women have orgasms for the first time, and since women now expect sexual pleasure, it makes sense they would buy sex toys. How do I buy sex products online without anyone finding out? If you want to protect yourself, look for that assurance, and make sure you're dealing with a real business, one that has a phone number, address, and contact information.

What about erotic literature? Until about 20 years ago, there wasn't the kind of female erotica that we have now. I think women read erotica to get in a sexy mood, but they don't get so excited that they masturbate. Is it true that women are now selling sex aids the way they used to sell tupperware?

At least 10,000 Passion parties are held month in private homes. The products that encourage foreplay are the most popular. These includes edible lotion, apple cinnamon, flavored body powder, and white chocolate flavored body pudding. Women want love and romance. With so much information and so many products on the market, are there areas of sexuality that we still don't know about? There's a lot about the chemistry, physiology, and neurology of female sexual response that we still don't understand very well. It's kind of shocking.

All our attention has focused on women who manifest too little libido, but I've identified a condition I call persistent arousal syndrome: A woman experiences constant arousal without conscious feelings of desire, which can go on for days, weeks, even months. despite orgasms. We also haven't paid much attention to the fact that" normal" women's sexual responses differ enormously. Some can have an orgasm of vibratory stimulation, and even then they say their orgasm is muted. Can you be happy without sex?

As a sex therapist, I can tell you that when a couple who haven't been sexually active suddenly have a good experience, you can see the difference. They come in laughing and talking; there's more physical affection between them. It's better than any therapy session. And there are more sexiess marriages than you think, relationships that can be bonded, loving, companionable, and devoted. Single women may find that what they most miss is a close relationship, not sex, and they find that closeness with friends.

That's why women do so well alone. What's the real story on midlife sex? Sex isn't the same at 50 as it is at 20, but neither is anything else. We finally going public with the fact that men go through a midlife transition, too, characterized by change of body shape, loss of muscle tone, and reduced sex drive. They need help achieving erections, and they may lose erections halfway through intercourse. Mad, passionate love will come and go at this age, but you can still have fun, unquote. Love is and I quote, according to the Bible, Though I speak with the tongues of men and of angels, but have not love, I have become sounding brass or a clanging cymbal. And though I have the gift of prophecy, and knowledge, and though I have all faith, so that I could remove mountains, but have not love, I am nothing.

And though I bestow all my goods to feed the poor, and though I give my body to be burned, but have not love, it profits me nothing. Love suffers long and is kind; love does not envy; love does not parade itself, is not puffed up; Does not behave rudely, does not seek it own, is not provoked, thinks no evil; Does not rejoice in iniquity, but rejoices in the truth; Bears all things, believes all things, hopes all things, endures all things.

Love never fails. But whether there are prophecies, they will fail; whether there are tongues, they will cease; whether there is knowledge, it will vanish away. For we know in part and we prophesy in part. And now abide faith, hope, love, these three; but the greatest of these is love, unquote.

Lets talk about the tongue and see how it relates to relationships, love, sex, and marriage. According to Theodore H. Epp, and I quote, God shows how that in every way a person expresses himself he does evil and not good and is unprofitable instead of profitable.

God begins with a person's tongue."Their throat is an open sepulchre' with their tongues they have used deceit; the poison of asps is under their lips: whose mouth is full of cursing and bitterness" (Rom. 3:13, 14). A person's tongue (his speech) indicates the condition of his heart. Jesus said," But those things which proceed out of the mouth come forth from the heart; and they defile the man. For out of the heart proceed evil thoughts, murders, adulteries, fornications, thefts, false witness, blasphemies" (Matt. 15: 18, 19). A person expresses his thoughts and his intentions through his tongue.

The tongue is like a valve that erupts under pressure, and the resulting explosion shows what is in the heart. James dealt with the boasteth great things. Behold, how great a matter a little fire kindleth! And the tongue is a fire, a world of iniquity: so is the tongue among our members, that it defileth the whole body. and setteth on fire the course of nature; and it is set on fire of hell" (James 3:5, 6).

The unregenerate person's mouth is a cesspool of ungodliness, swearing, cursing, slandering, gossiping (see Rom 3:14). Perhaps you have no problem with swearing or cursing, but what about slandering and gossiping? Slandering is tearing down the character of another. Gossiping is passing on information about others without concern for accuracy or f or the harm it might do to them.

Although these things are characteristic of the unregenerate, we who know Christ is Saviour must constantly be on guard so that we do not fall into the ways of the world. In this verse God is not telling what man does but what man is.

Because man is what he is, he does those things listed in Romans 3. In this section of Romans, God described, through the Apostle Paul, the speech of a person as having four different places of origin, the throat, the tongue, the lips and the mouth. The conversation of the average unregenerate person is repulsive to us; how much more abhorrent it must be to God, who cannot even think evil! Even after a person becomes a Christian, it is extremely difficult for him to control his tongue. The feet are described, he said, God says," Their feet are swift to shed blood: destruction and misery are in their ways" (Rom. 3:15, 16). Sin is lawlessness, and it is this lawlessness which is responsible for many of the horrible sins being committed today.

We're seen how eagerly people will shed blood in the unjust wars that have been raged, and we've seen the destruction of life that followed. The way of peace have they not know: there is no fear of God before their eyes" are the words of God uses to climax this particular description of man's evil ways (Rom. 3: 17, 18).

Sinful people do not find the way of peace through natural means. People must have personal peace before we can expect to have national peace. To the believer, Jesus said," Peace I leave with you, my peace I give unto you: not as the world giveth, give I unto you. People's basic problem, the root cause of all their trouble, is that they do not know God, and they do not fear meeting God when they die.

People speak lightly of death because they do not want to face its realities. People have taken it for granted that God, if He even exists, will overlook what they do and will take care of them regardless of how they live. People's refusal to make God the God of their lives is the fountain from which all these evils flow, unquote.

When you think about hate or families hating families it tends to throw a rug over the relationship in which you are involved. It dampers the relationship because you love that person so much and want that person in your life to be love by your family. You thought maybe one day that everything would changed from love to hate, and for whatever reasons it doesn't make senses. So lets talk about this hate family relationship by Richard Nicastro, and I quote as he enlighten us with his views and respect on such an outrageous problem. Marrying into a family he said is both true and not true. Certainly, when you join your life to someone else's, the things that are important to him become important to you, too. And family is at the top of the list. Just because you see his mother as a three headed guard dog doesn't mean he sees her that way. However, it's important to remember that you and your spouse, in getting married, have begun your own family. And for most people, that new family healthily takes precedent over the other. When both families are living in harmony, no one gives much thought to a loose sort of co-existence.

But when personalities clash. it might feel like your in laws are there with you all the time in the bedroom, in the kitchen while you attempt your first souffle, in the family room when your insist that your child observe her bedtime But Grandma say you make me go to bed too early!. Despite all the tension that can arise between the spouse and the in laws, most people agree that even the most Attila the Hun in laws aren't reason enough to abandon your betrothed at the altar.

As with almost any aspect of this he said Tilt a Whirl we call life, level headed examination and a fresh perspective can do wonders. If you examine your feelings from a safe distance, safely removed in time from the situation your in laws last destroyed or, better yet, thousands of miles and a couple of continents removed from the in laws themselves, you might see that it's not really hate that you're feeling, but rather strong annoyance, heavy dislike, or the I wouldn't want to ask them out for drinks or outlet shopping syndrome.

They may be sweet, loving and appropriate boundaries and the core issue is that you feel your spouse is overly connected to them, that he loves them or idealizes them too much. Jealousy can masquerade as righteous indignation. Another crucial thing to remember, you can't change someone else's behavior. You can't. No matter how gallantly you try, no matter how much those people need changing. The only behavior you are in complete control of is your own. You can only change how you react to people. And many times your new behavior shifts the dynamic enough so that it either forces or coaxes people to respond differently, in a way that squeezes out the behavior that originally made you pull your hair out.

You need to set healthy limits he said and acceptable boundaries around your marriage. It's easier to do this early in the marriage, before patterns have become entrenched. The irony is that sometimes you don't fully realize a situation needs an overhaul until you've lived with it for a while and until it feels unbearable. The first step is asking your spouse for help in approaching your in laws, after all, they're his/her parents and s/he has a history with them, one that should make communication easier and more fluid.

However, your mate might think this is all your problem. Time and time again, you might hear," I don't know what you're talking about, my parents are super! Without accusation or name calling, try hard with this one, communicate your feelings about your in laws to your spouse. Use specific examples rather than general feelings, and try to get your mate to walk even a few baby steps in your shoes. After all, s/he is in the middle and in the unenviable position between a rock and a hard place and getting squeezed; s/he loves the parents, love the spouse, and has to somehow mediate these warning factions.

You need to advocate for yourself with your in laws. Arrange a time for a chat. And call it that" chat". Try to voluntarily include your in laws in situations that feel palatable. For instance, you're organizing photo albums, and you'd love to put baby pictures of your spouse with your children's. Through it all, try to remember that, just as you feel a connection to your spouse, they have a connection to that same person.

They may feel more vulnerable than you do in face of your mate's new life, a life where you are now central and they are marginalis, unquote. Lets talk about insults and how insults affects a relationship.

Knowing and understanding the word and the danger of using such language just might save and strength your relationship. Here is an article by Rosiehorner, and I quote, Men please listen to this especially women, An insult is a statement or action, and I quote, when affronts or demeans someone. An insult may be intentional or accidental. Insults hurts. Sometime and I quote, folks just don't want to or too tired to find another way of speaking to someone.

When there is disappointment in a mate's behavior the person may, instead of pointing out the behavior, attempt to attack the person. Such as," Your are a poor excuse for a man." This was said by a woman feeling frustrated with her husbands recent behavior. Is there ever any truth? Insults often have some truth in them, that's why they hurt so much. The most dangerous kind of insults is the sneaky ones.

Those are insults that are disguised by good body language and tone of voice, unquote. Anger & Relationships—What You Need to Know, by Allen Thompson, and I quote, People get angry when they feel they been treated unfairly. When a person feels he has been treated unfairly he will get angry. If he feels he has been treated unfairly, he won't. It's as simple as that.

The important thing here is not what happens to the person, but his" feeling" or" perception" that he has been treated a certain way. Whether he has, in fact, been treated unfairly or not is irrelevant. As long as he thinks he has been treated unfairly he'll get angry, regardless of the situation, the outcome, or what happens to him. Such as sleeping with your girlfriend, making fun of your shirt, drink all your beer, kick your dog. But if you think you've been treated fairly, that you somehow deserves all this, then you won't get angry. You will remain calm and stoic. You may not like it very much, but you won't get angry. If two people spend any significant amount of time together, eventually there's going to be some anger.

A little bit every now and then. It's inevitable. How those two people with that anger will determine the course of the relationship. Will they break up? Will they stay together? Will they repress their feelings and wind up resenting one another? Or will they deal effectively with the anger... and perhaps become even closer as a result? Let's take a look at a few real-world examples of anger in action. and how to manage our thought and behaviors in order to convey that So Suave, Donjuanish image that we so desire. Say, for example, your girlfriend is angry with you. Very angry. She's banging pots, slamming cabinets, and giving you the evil eyes.

If you were like most guys you'd be nervous, irritated, confused, and maybe a little upset yourself. And you'd, very likely, be completely clueless as to what could set her off. And, an important point, her anger would most likely fuel your own anger toward her. As you don't understand why she's so mad, you yourself come to feel that YOU are being treated unfairly. But, of course, YOU are not like most guys— you're a freakin Don Juan.

You understand that her anger is caused by her perception that she was somehow treated unfairly (by you, or maybe by someone else). Now I'm not a big fan of giving conventional advice, and I very rarely suggest using logic with women... not male logic anyhow. (Remember that women are emotional creatures.) And you should very rarely discuss the" relationship process" with women. INTENT, is an important mediator of anger. It's very difficult to maintain anger at someone if treating you unfairly was not their intent. If you feel that your lady has somehow treated you unfairly, you can calmly explain the cause of your anger to her. Explain exactly what it is that makes you feel you've been treated unfairly.

She at this point will most likely apologize claiming that was not her intent. Once you point this out, it's her obligation to not do those things anymore (assuming you're not being unreasonable). Now this may sound like pretty simple stuff, but very often we don't understand the cause of our own anger.

Now, as a side not e, don't make the mistake of confusing Real Anger (this article) with False Anger. False anger does not follow the same rule and does not stem from the same underlying causes. For example, your lady might get angry and throw a little hissy fit in order to TEST you. to see how you respond. She wants to find out if you'll be a man and stand up for yourself, or if you'll be a little weenie boy and beg her for forgiveness? (Hint: you don't want to be the weenie boy.)

Or she might become angry simply to add a little drama and

excitement to a relationship which has become boring and mundane. As a Don Juan, it's your job to maintain the relationship, to keep the excitement levels high. So if she's resorting to false anger and other drama-inducing behaviors, then you're most likely not doing your job very well.

(Or, on the other hand, she could just be a nut!)You might be pleasantly surprised at how an understanding of anger can positively impact your life by helping you to better understand your feelings in a variety of situations. Many of these guys are angry. They're angry at women. They often feel that women are illogical, stupid, or just plain mean. They don't understand women... AT ALL. Now let me point out here that anger is not always destructive. In fact, sometimes it can actually serve useful purposes. Have you ever wondered why some women stay in relationships with abusive men... While other women leave, file charges, or cut peckers off and toss them out car windows?

It has a lot to do with anger and the woman's perception that she is either being treated fairly or unfairly. The women who stay in these relationships tend to have very low self-esteem. And thus, they don't see the abusive behavior as being unfair treatment. They, for some reason, feel as though they deserve the mental and/or physical abuse.

And without that critical perception of unfairness, and without the anger that results, they don't have the necessary motivation to make a change. On the other hand, women with high self-esteem will get angry when they are treated in an abusive fashion. They don't feel as though the behavior is warranted or fair. And they will take steps to change the situation.

The key here is having complete control over your anger response so as not to say or do something stupid that you'll wind up regretting later. Don't let anger control you or interfere in your relationships. Take charge. Be a man, unquote.

Stress in Relationships, by Katt Chat, and I quote, Through many couples experience problems during the course of their relationships, it is according to her often how they deal with those problems that will either keep them together or, break them apart. A true she said of love and respect is how people treat each other when problems arise and as difficult as it might be to remain respectful toward a person that has become such a comfortable fixture in a persons life, this constant upkeep can allow for the happiest of couples, even in the worst o f times. Many people feel that relationships today undergo a great deal of stress for many reasons; the changing roles of men and woman; our fast paces society she said; both partners having careers while trying to raise a family and many more reasons that can be seen in modern day relationships.

One of the most she said difficult aspects of these problems is that in order to resolve them the couple need time together. Too many people find that even while living under the same roof she said they don't have the time to pour into lengthy discussions and when they do it seems a waste of the precious little time they have together because they perceive it as a negative.

Unfortunately, not attending the underlying problems that a couple may have will not resolve them; instead she said they are often brought up during other arguments; cause other problems that seem unfixable because the source isn't being addressed; or simply cause the couple to live in a state of unhappiness because they both know that something is wrong. Thought it does require participation she said, getting to the heart of the problem does not require dwelling on it for hours at a time.

In fact, she said, a wonderful way to prepare for an important discussion is to write down your personal thoughts about it, points that you would like to cover, on your own time; this will for a great deal more time focused on the issues rather than wasting time trying to think of key points.

A few basic recommendations before you sit down: Write down your most important points so that you do not become flustered and forget. Pick a time that is convenient for both you and your partner which allows you all the time you may need. One basic problem that seems to occur in many relationships she said is the routine act of taking each other for granted. This can apply to hundreds of daily tasks and activities that become habit after enough time has gone by. Taking the time to thank your partners she said for the effort that they put into the relationship is extremely important.

Quite often, a little attention and praise can go a long way toward creating a happy environment. Constantly feeling underappreciated can cause a great deal of unnecessary stress; in many cases one partner will have no ideal that the other is having these feelings.

While it is the responsibility she said of both partners to appreciate each other, it is also important to express any feelings which might not be apparent.

A regular argument amongst couples is that one partner should have known that the other partner was unhappy; while it is good to remain attentive to how your partner is feeling; if a problem is going unnoticed she said it becomes the responsibility of that person to voice it so that together, the couple can figure out how to solve it.

Many people choose to keep feelings she said or thoughts to themselves because they either have no wish to bother their partner, or would like to see their partner recognize that the problem exists without their help. Though it is understandable she said this kind of action often causes more problems and leads to a pattern of behavior that divides the couple, rather than allowing them to get closer.

Safety in Relationships by Home Health Guides, and I quote, In healthy relationships, there is respect and honesty between both people. This means that you listen to each other's thoughts and opinions and accept each other's right to say no or to change your mind without giving each other a hard time. Communication is also important in healthy relationships. You should be able to let the other person know how you are feeling. You might disagree or argue sometimes, but in healthy relationships you should be able to talk things out together to reach a compromise that works for both of you. Be honest and tick to your decision.

Tell your partner you like spending time with him or her but that you also want to spend time with others and family. In a healthy relationship, you both need time to hang out with friends as well as time for yourselves. In a risky or unhealthy relationship, you usually feel the exact opposite of how you feel when you're in a" healthy relationship".

You and your partner do not usually feel good about each other and yourselves. Not all unhealthy relationships are abusive but sometimes they can include violence or abuse, verbal, physical, emotional, or sexual. This can involve both people being violent or abusive toward each other or can involve only one person doing this to the other. Many times, a relationship is not unhealthy in the very beginning, but over time abusive behavior might show.

You may feel afraid or pressured to do something that you don't want to do. There are many signs that you could be in an abusive or unhealthy relationship. Is jealous or possessive of you, he or she gets angry when you talk or hang out with other friends or people of the opposite sex. bosses you around, makes all the decisions, tell you what to do. tell you what to wear, who to talk to, where you can go. is violent to other people. gets in fights a lot. loses his/her temper a lot, pressures you to have sex or to do something sexual that you don't want to do. swears at you or uses mean language. blames you for his or her problems, tell you that it is your fault that he or she hurt you, insults you or tries to embarrass you in front of other people. has physically hurt you, and makes you feel scared of their reactions to things. An abusive relationship may include any of the signs listed. Physical abusive, is when a person touches your body in an unwanted or violent way.

This may include hitting, slapping, punching, kicking, pulling, biting, choking, or using a weapon on you. Verbal / Emotional Abuse, is when a person says something or does something that makes you afraid or feel bad about yourself. This may include: yelling, name-calling, saying mean things about your family and friends, embarrassing you on purpose, telling you what you can and can't do, or threatening to hurt you or hurt themselves.

Blaming you for their problems, or verbally pressuring you to use drugs or alcohol, or keeping you from spending time with friends and family. Sexual Abuse, is any sexual contact that you do not want. You may have said no or may be unable to say no because the abuser has threatened you or prevented you from saying no.

This may include forcing you to have sex or unwanted touching or kissing. After a person is violent, he or she may apologize and promise never to hurt you again, and even say that they will work on the relationship. It may be a while before that person acts violent again.

These ups and downs can make it hard to leave a relationship. Abusive relationships are very unhealthy for you. You can have trouble sleeping or have headaches or stomach aches. You might feel depressed, sad, anxious, and you may even lose or gain weight.

You may also blame yourself, feel guilty, and have trouble trusting other people in your life. Staying in an abusive relationship can hurt your self-confidence and make it hard for you to believe in yourself. First, if you think that you are in a unhealthy relationship, you should talk to a parent, friend. Counselor, doctor, teacher, coach or other trusted person about your relationship. Loneliness Affects Brain Activity And Social Behavior, by eNotAlone.com and I quote, Researches have revealed over the time that loneliness leads to decreased activation of the ventral striatum.

The ventral striatum is a region of the brain associated with taking the perspective of another person is much less activated among lonely individuals compared with the ones that do not consider themselves as lonely. The experts found out that individuals who reported being bored and experienced dullness in their marriages at year seven had a greater decrease in marital satisfaction at year sixteen.

According to the investigators those couples who were not bored after 7 years of living together, experienced a typically small decrease in marital satisfaction after 16 years of relationship. They recommend that married couple go out for a night date on a weekly basis, in which they better do something together that they have never or rarely done before, something that is not just enjoyable, but in some way exciting, unquote.

You have addressed important issues and concerns of love, and relationships, but it's also important to understand that not all relationships end up in disaster. In all relationships it what you make it. "It's not easy". To say it is, I would be lying. If you can understand the important of what you do or don't do, there would probably be less broken relationships and marriages. When relationship are broken, destroyed, ruin, who do we blame? First and foremost it's usually ourselves, and secondly the other person or persons involved in the relationship. It could even be our parent, children, friends, and other people. When relationships falls apart the blame scatters affecting everyone involved. Yes, it could be ugly. Why? Because the person is hurting. The pain is severe and tearing the person mentally, psychologically, physically, and emotionally apart. Digging into the deepness of the person sole. Eating that person alive. Its almost like being physically torture until the pain stops. The list is usually long and unlimited.

What usually happens next? Yes, its excuses. We start making excuses for ourselves. It's enough to make you wonder. It's enough to make you think. All this time your thinking, and under the impression that these people have a good relationship, a good marriage. Think about this. Not all relationships or marriages ends up in disaster. But love is blind.

You determines the life span and future of your relationship with each other. It doesn't take a brain or the smartest person in this world we live in to comprehend and understand that. You hear people talking about their relationships and their marriages all the time. What does it mean? Is it important or is it not? Never speak badly of the dead because the dead can't help you. You destroyed your relationship and your marriage. You have no one to blame but yourself. The question is, what are you going to do about it?

We have seen and witnessed even the best of relationships and marriages fall apart. If your marriage or relationship is in trouble why not fix it before the walls starts thumbing down. If there is no solvable solution why remain in that marriage or relationship? Why not end it peacefully? "Just walk away". Why stay in a relationship or a marriage and end up in total destruction? Be smart, leave in peace. Give the person time to calm down. To re-collect their thoughts and their peace of mind. Sometime giving them or that person space will solve the problem. The expression is," just give me space". That word" space", means a lot. We need to take the time, give ourselves a time out and digest that word. We need to determine exactly what is means in term of relationships and marriage. Because it takes two to have a relationship and two to have a marriage. When hurting, the other one hurts.

This is an assumption of course that you both feels the same way respectfully with love and tenderness of emotions. Have you ever thought about one day just one day that you will get back together? Never rule out that possibility because it could happen. Its like saying don't give up the ship until it sinks. Don't ever jump to the conclusion that a relationship or a marriage is over. Don't mistakenly misread the signs. Its not over until its over. Don't assume its over because things look bad. The grass is greener on the other side. "Never ever assume". Don't let your feelings and emotions misguide you, causing you to do and say the wrong thing. Never act irrationally. Think before you act and put the best foot forward to achieve a successful ending of whatever the problem might be hounding and hindering your relationship or marriage."If its not broken don't fix it, but if it is broken" get with it" and don't stop until you fix it.

Sometime a woman would say that's something you should be telling yourself. You can argue it because their right. A woman know when she's right. She will not hastate to tell you when your wrong. Some marriages and relationships ends up bad, death of the entire family or one person killing the other. Why, why, why, because if I can't have you, no one will. If you don't love me anymore, find your dead. This is no joke. This is no laughing matter. Its true. It doesn't stop there. One that cheats on the other. Again, ask yourself questions. What did I do to cause all of this? How can I stop what is happening? What can I do different? What if anything I can do to save this relationship, to save this marriage?

What leads us to this point? Why did this person killed his family, children, and himself? A relationship between a man and a woman is something special. Its like sucking a sugar daddy. The more you suck it the sweeter it get. The longer your into a relationship the stronger it grows. Once a relationship begins to grow, grow in strength, and in unity, it gets stronger, and therefore very hard, and very difficult to let go. Again, don't let your emotions and feelings cause you to do and say the wrong thing. A life is special and precious.

Never dune yourself to hail but walk in the light. Hurting and painful situations, and problems can cause you to say and do the wrong thing, and by the time you think about it its too late. Anger can cause you to say and do the wrong thing. Can we learn from others mistakes?

Yes, of course we can. If that's true and of course it is then why is history repeating itself? Why are there senseless killings and the taking of innocent lives? Is having a relationship with another person important? Well, you be the judge of that. After all you're the person in question. What roll does the man play in the relationship and in a marriage? What roll does the woman play? If you say sex your wrong. Sex is important in a relationship and in a marriage, and more so in a marriage due to the type of relationship you have. Its not just a boy friend or a girl friend thing. Because marriage is about each other and hopefully one day having a family. You are the extension of lives to come. Families and future families to be in order that our world will remain strong as it carries out the tradition of relationships. Although sex is important in all relationships especially marriages. The man is the fore runner of the relationship and in a marriage. He's the head and the footprint of the relationship and in a marriage. He therefore determines the future of the relationship and of course the marriage. The man is seen as the most important person in the relationship and in a marriage but the woman is equally important.

The woman depends on the man to structure the relationship and in a marriage. The man is like the engine of a train. He must be able to set directions of the relationship and for the marriage. He must be able to change directions of the relationship and for the marriage. He must know when to jump tracks in terms of seeking help from others. He must know that no man is an island and no man stands alone. He therefore must be able to recognize the signs of trouble and willing to seek help.

This all makes sense and will determine the future of your relationship and your marriage. "Be the man and stop being the fool". Don't let your pride get in the way of loosening the one you love and cares so much about. Do what you need to do to save your relationship and your marriage to the bitter end even if it means opening up yourself to total embarrassment. Sometime being the man you must do what you must do. Even if it means walking away from a relationship or a marriage. You can sometime save a relationship and a marriage just by doing that. Not in all cases but you can say you tried. Trying is half the battle. You may have lost your pride but you gain her respect. To do something is better than doing nothing. Its better than saying nothing. Saying something does make a different on how a woman feels. You could change a negative attitude into a positive."Just watch the body language". A woman slapping you doesn't mean that she hate you. She could be telling you I love you. Lets get busy. Meaning it time to do the wild thing. Lets make love. But be careful not to misread the signs. Because its also a time when a woman is letting her anger and frustration out.

She could be venting. It is also a time when a woman is expressing anger, and disappointment in you and that happens. Sometime you can't be sure unless of course you know the woman and aware of what's going on. Sometime you still can't be sure. What is the normal expression? I thought I knew you. You really surprise me. All these years I have been sleeping with a stranger. You sorry piece of trash. You bastard. Surely, these expressions are very familiar to you, and of course there are others. The list doesn't stop. A woman believe it or not can think of plenty.

What should you do when this happens? Whatever you do be courteous, polite, sincere, and respectful toward her feelings, emotions and stress. Because problems can and will cause stress. Stay in control of your feelings, emotions, and the situation. You don't necessary has to mean it but it happens, and when it does it can really piss you off.

Its like getting a shock treatment and not knowing what to do. What about I'm sorry honey despite everything I still love you. Don't be too quick to approach her or to hug her especially when she's angry. Watch carefully the body language. Let the body language and her respond dictate what you do. Although its true some women can push you to a point of no return, and will try to force you to do the unthinkable. That is putting your hands on them when you really don't want to do so. They do it out of anger and out of spike to cause you to do the wrong thing, and then start insulting and putting you down, and that's not right. Women have their way of turning things around making you look like the bad guy. There is good and bad in everyone and evil does not stand alone. Don't just stand there and do nothing unless of course you don't love or care about the relationship or the marriage.

But again that's a horse with a different tail. But if you do care about the relationship and the marriage do something even if you are at fault. Why is that so important? It tell the woman you care or the man that I love you. I want our relationship and our marriage to work. I don't want to loose you. Your very important to me. You're my everything. You're the grass I walk on. You're my cup runic over with love.

I will do anything to keep us together."Just name it". I will jump over a pile of hot coals for you. I will bathe you and kiss your feet. Anything, whatever it takes to save what we have, and that's each other. Be sincere, be honest with your feelings and emotions, and truthful. Don't say something that you don't mean. A woman knows when your lying. Don't try to play her or make a fool out of her. Women don't like that.

Remember this, its not what you say, its how you say it. Tears of another person will sometime cause you to cry. Its that normal, yes or no? Yes of course. Is it a sign of weakness? No, not in all situations. The woman is usually the first to cry. Is that normal? Yes. Is it ok for a man to cry? Yes, of course. But a man will usually try to avoid crying. A man should not cry when he know that a woman will use it against him."The expression is, he always cries. At the same token some women will get upset if the man don't cry at some point in a relationship. Women see this as being cold and heartless. In other words, you have no feelings. They will use it against you. They will turn and say why am I with you? Why did you get married in the first place? You should be by yourself. Women have a way of making you feel like a dog."Be that as it may".

What roll does women play in a relationship and in a marriage? Women plays many rolls. What is the most important roll a woman plays? Let look at her in this respect. A woman is your friend, companion, and your lover. Her key roll is support. She is there to support you in all that you do. But she's not there to be ordered around or to be your slave or to be control by you. She is not there to take your foolishness or to be beaten and physically abuse.

She is like your side kick, your spare tire, your second wheel, or if you would she's there supporting you. She is not trash, or a piece of wood, and she's not a thing or an object that you pushes around. She is a person with feelings and emotions. She is a human being but most importantly she's a woman. She is a person with a heart and has blood running throughout her body providing life twenty four hours a day. She's someone special and being such she has the ability to give birth, a life, and carry it for nine months."Can you"? Of course not.

So treat her with respect, love, and with sincerity. No man, no man is capable of doing such a thing and never will. When a woman doesn't respect herself it break down the barrel of the relationship and the marriage. When that happens all kind of problems sets in. Its not just anger which is usually follow by violent. It causes a disregard or a lack of thought if you would for the relationship and for the marriage and for the family as a unit. Her lack of concern and dissuades or opinionated attitude can and will display unwillingly the wrong message, causing a volcano eruption of the relationship and the marriage. It's not hard or difficult to loose sight of what's important. But to understand the problem and why a woman does what she does, performs and acts the way she does you'll need to understand the woman.

Women belief is far, far, different from men."That's a good thing". How are they different? They can biologically and physically give birth and carry that life of a child for nine months. Women are considered more mature in nature due to the development of their brain in term of age of maturity then men. Does that make them smarter? Not necessary. Its just a scientific belief that women are smarter then men given their age of maturity.

Lets take a look at this word, phrenology, and I quote, which is the study of the shape and irregularities of the human skull, base on the now discredited belief that they reveals character and mental capacity, unquote. With all that said and the study of the brain. That theory would support that a woman is more mature then a man. Women obviously dress differently then men.

There is no argument there. Isn't that good? What if anything are they trying to tell or dictate to man? Is it important for women to dictate what she feels a man should do or not to do? Is it her right. Is it her place? What do you think? Is she trying to be more then just a woman? What precautions if any would you suggest or would you wait until the relationship has came to a point of destruction?

What if a woman strangely tell you that you must do this and you must do it right now or else. How would that make you feel? How would you respond to her? Should you respond then or wait until later giving yourself time to think about what has been said? Women have a way of testing you and its their way of bringing out the man in you and maybe even the beast. It's a show of strength and weakness. It makes you wonder for instant whose wearing the pants. If you really think about it what different does it makes? Does it makes a different? How you respond to a woman is very important. Its not necessary when. Do it within a reasonable time that way she want feel as if you are ignoring her.

That could cause some unpleasant reactions and unwanted problems if you will that you don't need. Don't be easily lead or control by a woman. Surprise, yes it does happens. Why should a relationship come to that one controlling the other? It makes you feel being incarcerated like a prisoner within your own body. It's a feeling of entrapment. Surely that is not putting it too harshly. The bottom line is women like to feel in control. It is not about sex.

Don't be blindly thinking that way. It could back and kick you in the ass. Don't think for a second that you understand a woman. You will never be able to understand a woman. A woman have mood swings that you'll never be able to comprehend or understand. That's what makes a woman a woman. A woman will enlighten you by displaying her feelings and emotions when she feels that you are ready to accept them sending you a message of hope and understanding.

Women simply wants to be treated equal. But more importantly like a woman. They don't mind being in control. But treat them like a woman. Don't treat them like a second class citizen. Show them they are important to you. Show them that you care and you love them. Say the sweetest thing to them."Move the lips and let the words come out".

When you respond passionately a woman will say that was very sweet of you, that was really nice of you, Let not go out lets go to bed, and of course I love you. Women are more open with their feelings then men. Women are more easily to cry. That can sometime intimidate a man. Damn I wish she wouldn't cry.

What does she wants now? Or it could make him feel more affections? It can make him grab hold of his heart, feeling and emotions, and say you know what, I really love this woman. Its almost like letting yourself go. Letting the love show. Dissecting the real you and without feeling foolish. Women are more quickly to make a fool out of themselves. Why do they do it? Most of the time to get your attention. Why do a woman dresses a certain way and putting on a pretty face? To get your attention. To look good for you. To make you feel pride of them. Maybe she's simply feeling good. Maybe she's showing you just how sexy she can really be, and sexually arousing. Maybe just to see how you will react. Its not her harmonies running wild. How you respond depends on what's going on at the moment.

When you do respond do it in a sincere and loving way making her feel like a woman, and most importantly like she's special to you. Raise the bar if you will addressing her. Men its called sweet talk. Lets talk about sex. Is sex important in a relationship and in a marriage?

How important is sex? How often should you have sex? Who should initiate sex? Does it matters? Believe it or not this word no matter how small or simple it may appear can hurt and destroy your relationship, your marriage and even your life. This simple word "sex" is a very powerful word. So I asked you again, is sex important in a relationship and in a marriage?

Yes it is. Sex is mental and physical. Sex can also be emotional. You can't live without each other. You dreams constantly about each other."Wanting that person". You must have that person in your life. What happens when the sex slowly stops or its only when the other person wants it? That could pose some serious problems, issues, and concerns.

It can also destroy the relationship and the marriage. It can invite demoniac into your relationship and marriage. It can invite others, outsiders into your relationship and marriage. Share equally and have sex but do it with respect for each other. Do it because you love that person. Sex is good. Sex is pleasure. It's the act of pleasing each other sexually. Its telling that person I love and cares about you. There is nothing wrong with having sex if perform within the decency of the relationship and of course the marriage. Who said that you must have sex everyday, every hours, or even every week? You and the person within your relationship, and your emotions and feelings determines when or if you should have sex. Is there a special time to have sex? No, and that's what's good about it.

Have sex when your harmonies is going crazy and wants it. It's a spare of the moment thing happening within you. You know what I'm talking about."Do it now. Can you imagine how good that will be? Who said that you must have sex at all? Don't have sex because you know she's going to be expecting. Don't put a time on when to have sex."Just do it and enjoy it". Don't do it for the wrong reason. Men and women tends to make the mistake we must have sex now, we must have it today, we must have it tonight, and I must have sex all the time. Wrong, wrong, wrong. Wrong answer.

Don't do this to yourself and most importantly don't do it to the other person. Again, don't plan to have sex. Its not a date. Its not a job. Your body will tell you when it needs sex and wants it. Women you have ways of making the men want you and to want to have sex."Don't You"? Men don't you try this. Its not the same.

Women are naturally very attracted and strongly very sexy. The way in which a woman dresses and her body language will tell you a lot, such as she's in the mood, she's not, and lastly stay away from me. Men, its not what a woman wears its how she wears it. That's the dammit thing they know how to get your attention. There is no limit to what a woman can wear. A woman will do what she needs to do to look good. A woman likes to feel good. A woman likes to feel sexy. More importantly a woman likes to feel sexually attracted to her man. In other words men, she's trying desperately to please you. She wants you men to feel turn on by her. Hot pants were once the most talk about things at one time."Too much ass was showing".

I think now" Tight Pants" has taken over. It has nothing to do with how they look. Its how they make you feel. Short skirts have taken the place of Mini Skirts. Thank God for that. They were definitely too short. They left nothing to the imagination. The short skirts are not so bad. A woman looks very sexy wearing them and it leave something to the imagination. Short skirts are in and they are sexy. Men eat your heart out. What make sex good? What make sex wonderful? It's the two of you wanting it and craving for it emotionally and sexually. Your relationship and marriage depends strongly on sexually fulfillment and you satisfying each other.

What about sex toys? If sex toys and sexual videos can help kinder your relationship and your marriage by all means have fun. Don't let money get in the way of your love for each other, don't let work get in the way, and above all have time for sex and each other.

Your marriage and your relationship depends on it. Don't do it because you feel that you must do it. Don't do it out of fear. Sex is personal. Sex is something special if you partake for the right reasons. When only the other person wants it is not a good reason to have sex. Its not a pretty picture. Gang banging is not a pretty picture. Prostitution is not a pretty picture.

Rape is not a pretty picture."Shout No". This is not what sex is. It's like violating the bura ground of the dead taking what's not yours by force and aggressively destroying the physical environment of the area.

Its like a volcano is about to erupt. It can and will become a very serious, and a very stressful psychological situation if the person doesn't seek help. It can and will destroy that relationship, marriage, and the family as well. Surely, we don't want that to happen. So what should we do? If the person your concerned about don't seek help then you be the" bigger person and seek help for that person. You could have just save that relationship. What if the person doesn't wants to go and seek help? If all else fails see if the professional is willing to come to your resident although it might cost you more.

If that professional attends the same church as you just maybe it could be done there setting a more comfortable environment making that person feel more relax. Finally, maybe the pastor could work with you and that person to hopefully make your relationship and marriage better. "No one else has to know". The person just might feel better doing it that way.

Because the pastor already know you. You don't feel like your being force to be there. You don't feel uncomfortable, and maybe the problem is something simple not serious at all. Maybe only serious to you. Now that we have talked about sex. Take if you will a deep breathe. Is there love without sex? According to a dear friend a woman I know sex is not love. Is there a different? Well, according to her there is.

You don't has to love someone to have sex with them. This is something we do each and everyday men and women alike throughout the United States and around the world."We have sex". Having sex is something we do. Its part of what make us human beings. Should you wait until your in love to have sex? Should you wait until your married to have sex?

Is it a sin to have sex before marriage? Before answering those questions. First of all what is love? According to the dictionary and I quote, Love is deep affection and warm feelings for another. The emotion of "sex" and romance, strong sexual desire for another person. A strong fondness or enthusiasm, unquote. You know when your in love its something obvious. Love is something that you can't hide, disguise, or pretend if your seriously in love. Because you can't and its very difficult to do. True love of affection, deep emotions and feelings will make you want to be with that person. It will cause you to do crazy things. You'll have sleepless nights. You'll come running wearing a coat naked from head to toe just to be with that person. Nothing will keep you apart" not even death".

What is sin? It is and I quote, A transgression of a religious or moral law. Something shameful, unquote. How does sin relates to sex? Sex becomes a sin when we sell ourselves for money or for the pure pleasure of sex such as prostitution, sexually related escort services, performing at private parties, sexually related clubs and bars, and publication of magazines as a means of making money.

Dirty money if you would having sex at such a young age and forcibly against their will.

How can we stop this? Is it a problem? There are many things that you can do such as education and law enforcement intervention and involvement.

How does adultery fits into all of this? First of all what is adultery? According to the dictionary and I quote, it is voluntary sexual intercourse between a married person and a partner other than the lawful spouse, also, to praise or admire excessively, fawn on, unquote.

We are all guilty of this. It will without warning destroy your relationship and your marriage and a family. The mere thinking about another person is considered an adultery. The cold staring at another person while thinking immoral thoughts is considered an adultery. Don't think it don't do it. Don't do it don't think it. Knowing that why do people do it? It human nature to think about sex. A beautiful woman. A sexual handsome man. Is it right? No. But it does happens. There are many reasons for doing it. Everybody have their own reasons for doing it. Such as he's too cold. He don't show me attention or enough of attention. He's not emotionally here for me. We don't have sex. He stop loving me. He doesn't sexually satisfied me in bed. We have no sex. No fore play. No kissing, touching, hugging, or words of sweetness. He just jump on and jump off. "Takes it like a dog". He has no money.

He's never home. He's not affections to me. He's in jail or incarcerated. He's too tired. He just wants to sleep. Never in the mood at least not for me. He abuse me physically and emotionally. He don't take me anywhere. We're always home. We never go anywhere or do anything. He want help cook. He spends too much time doing other things.

These are just some of the reasons or excuses people used when committing an adultery. What problems can it cause? Do we really has to ask? Of course not. If you has to ask then something is wrong. But its important to understand that others suffer when a relationship and a marriage is destroyed due to adultery. Everyone involved in the relationship or marriage suffers which also includes the children. Children suffers, broken homes, broken families. Sometime a relationship and a marriage can be save despite the situation.

The key word is "Sometime". Because its not true in all cases. Something as simple as a "lie' can destroy a relationship and a marriage. Where do we draw the line? How far do we go? There is no easy answer. There is no easy solution. But there is something called a second chance. There is something called repent and redemption. Which is according to the dictionary and I quote, repent: to feel remorse or regret for what one has done or failed to do, unquote. And redemption: In Christianity, salvation from sin through Jesus's sacrifice, unquote. There is something called forgiveness, and I 'm sorry. It all depends on you and how far you want to go. Do you still love that person? Do you still care for that person? Do you care and love that person enough to give that person a second chance? Its something that you will has to decide. No one can decide it for you. There are certain decisions that you as a person, as a man, and as a woman will have to make yourself. Again, do you care and love that person enough to give that person a second chance?

"What if", places doubts within you, and in your mind, causing you sometime to make the wrong decisions. It causes you to deny yourself the need and desires that you really want, and the decision that you must make. Don't second guess yourself. Know what you want. Don't let doubts destroy your happiness and to make the wrong decisions, such as what if, what if it was you, what if things were different, what if it happened to you, and other if's.

There are so many "What if". What if I blame you, what if I take you back, and what if nothing has changed? Where does it stop? What are we to do now? Thank God for Frank Vilassa who knows about love. According to Frank Vilaasa, who wrote What Is Love, and I quote, he said it is fair to say that much of the love we experience in our lives, both individually and collectively is unconscious.

We don't really know and appreciate the love we have for someone till they are gone—either to the other world, or to some other part of this world. As a society he said, our understanding about love is still limited—and this is especially true when it comes to relationships between men and women. He said you don't have to look very far to see that the male-female relationship is not functioning at its fullest potential in our society. A lot of ignorance about nature of love still exists, unquote. He said this ignorance has its roots in our society's traditional belief in the sanctity of marriage. For both religious and social reasons, our culture was always far more interested in keeping a marriage together, than it was in the well being of the two souls caught in the marriage. Marriage was like he said a marathon race—you had to run through the pain to get the prize. The actual process of cultivating love—how this was done—was given little attention.

Many people nowadays still consider longevity to the hallmark of a loving relationship. Love is still equated with commitment, unquote.

Lets turn our attention over to a word that has been verbally expressed a lot and transformed into action by many. Anger, not just anger, but anger and relationships. According to this article from the internet, and I quote, Unless we make a continuous effort to deal with anger as it arises, our relationship will suffer. Anger according to this article is particularly destructive in relationships. When we live in close contact with someone, our personalities, priorities, interests, and ways of doing things frequently clash.

Since we spend so much time together, and since we know the other person's shortcomings so well, it is very easy for us to become critical and short-tempered with our partner and to blame him or her for making our life uncomfortable. A couple may genuinely love one another, but if they frequently get angry with each other the time when they are happy together will become fewer and further between. Eventually there will come a point when before they have recovered from the row the next has already begun. A relationship in which there is a lot of friction and conflict of interests is also an unrivaled opportunity to erode away our self—cherishing and self—grasping, which are the real sources of our problems. It is through our anger and hatred that we transform people in enemies, Unquote. Case in point a relationship no matter how precious it may be encounters problems of immoral nature that will cause friction between you and your partner, and these are mostly problems that you unfortunately never thought would ever happen to you such as cheating. With that in mind lets talk about signs of cheating by Heidi Muller, and I quote, never underestimate a woman's willingness to stray 'women can be just as unfaithful as men in relationships.

Just the thought of your partner putting her paws on another man makes your skin crawl. That's why its always important to keep a lookout for some of the surefire signs you have a cheating partner. Many of the major signs you have a cheating partner is if you spot any changes your partner behavior. Small things you used to mess up aren't enraging your partner.

This could be a good thing. But it should make you wonder why your partner no longer cares. Your partner no longer shares daily events with you. When you asked your partner questions your partner turns the table on you. It's a sad fact but there is no such thing as a perfect relationship. There is always a chance that your partner might be cheating on you.

Women are typically detail-oriented; If she's cheating on you. You'll have to start paying attention. If your looking for a starting point for your detective work. The fact that she no longer wants to attend your family's functions or hang with your friends is one of our signs of cheating on you. Now, every sentiment you express sets her off and she finds any excuse to lash out at you. If she habitually begins to point out your every flaw, you may want to get to the bottom of what's really going on. When a mysterious friend inches his way into the picture.

If she gets defensive about disclosing information. In any relationship, there are good days and bad days. Now and again, however, your differences might become more serious and can lead to a breakup. These are signs of looming trouble, and when they are seen with some frequency, it might be time to cut your losses and end the relationship, unquote. Jealous, what a monster.

According to the dictionary, and I quote, an intolerant of viralry or unfaithfulness apprehensive of the loss of another's exclusive devotion. Jealousy, attitude or feeling. Jeopardy, exposure to or imminence of death, loss, or injury What does jealousy has to do with relationship and marriage? When a person is jealous what if anything comes to mind?

Mad a lot and taking it out on anyone, saying you did this and that, threatening to kill and pushing you around, cornering you like a dog, beating and yelling at you, yelling at the children and knocking things about, nothing you say or do is good enough, forcibly rapes you like an animal, and the list goes on, its unlimited. Does it affect the relationship and the marriage? It's a dangerous and a none healthy environment. I saw you talking to that person. What were you saying? What were you smiling about? Are you cheating on me?

What did he give you? Don't lie I saw you. These are warning signs people not something to ignore. Signs of jealousy which can hurt a relationship and a marriage. Don't get me wrong.

Being jealous is normal human behavior and reaction to what we see around us. But when it becomes a problem like the unmentionable described earlier, its more then just a problem, and it must be death with head on, immediately, because it can kill. It can cause lightening to stripe you dead leaving you on the ground to be eaten by dogs and carry off by the unknown.

We have seen this happened even on television and in various movies, and yes in real life. We wonder why these things happens. This is something that we live with and experience everyday in relationships and marriages. What makes a person jealous. If you care about the person and the relationship don't do it. Most times someone ends up getting hurt. We don't want these things to happen but they do. Think about the following: Baby you look good. Do your man know your out here? There is a party across the street, hey, come and have some fun. Yell baby your man want mine. Peace out baby show us what your talking about.

I saw you with, Why were you holding his hand, didn't I tell you not to go out? Why did you disobey me? I saw you dancing with him, What did you say?" You go to hell. I'm not good enough for you? Take off that dress, didn't I tell you not to wear it? Give it back. What should you do? Whatever you do be smart about it. Do not ignore the problem and yield to the warning signs. The red flags inside your head. Don't assume nothing is wrong.

Carefully and cautiously confront the person and if all possible have an escape plan of action.

Anything can happen. Things can get out of control. Always expect the worst. You above all try to stay calm and maintain control of the conversation and situation. Don't let the rival of the problem cause you to say or do the wrong thing. Stay in control.

If you feel its necessary and important enough tell someone, such as your best friend, parent, and maybe even your clergy. The other person doesn't has to know, Don't bloomer it out. Its putting fuel on the fire. We don't want that. It is not necessary and unwanted.

The most important thing is solving the problem. Again, yielding to the warning signs, if you know what makes the other person jealous, don't do it. If you fear for your life and personal safety, and the life of others, such as your children, by all means tell someone. Because now other lives are in danger, not just your own. Don't take jealousy for granted. Be aware of what jealousy is and can lead to. Lets talk about trust or truth regarding marriages and relationships. In a relationship especially a marriage you are expected to be honest and truthful with each other."Watch out now". You are expected. What does that really means? Be careful especially men. Don't walk into an entrapment. When a woman asked the question, how do you really feels bout me, about us? What do you think she's really asking?

Is she really asking you how you feel or is she asking you to lie? Men, don't walk into that question blindly, and if you do, have your bags packed or at least know where your going to sleep later. Remember, open mouth insert foot can cause a lot of unwanted problems."Think before you speak. Men, ask yourself a question. Was she really asking me for the truth?

Was that truly what she wanted to hear? Don't be foolish men. Whatever you do, walk into those questions with both eyes opened and mouth shut. Your respond men could haunt you for the rest of your life. Is this really how you feel? How long have you been feeling that way?

Why you never said anything before? You know what, shut the "F" up. Get out. Get out of my house. Get out of my car. You don't love me. I don't turn you on? I'm too what!

I'm not sexy enough for you? Your in love with who? The chemistry between us is gone. Damn, your nothing but a bastard. How dare you. He said what? Whatever you do always watch out for flying objects, and that deadly and vicious slap across the face. The truth men, if you really think about it is not what everyone wants to hear.

Their expecting to hear how much you love and cares about them. Nothing less. How does this affects your relationship and your marriage? If you have any respect for each other, and your relationship, and your marriage, don't walk into those questions blindly. Make damn sure that telling them the truth will not cause any problems between the two of you putting your marriage and relationship in jeopardy of being destroy. Fighting for your relationship, is an article written by Dan and Anne McMenamin, its very important for you to know and understand how they feel about relationships as it relates to real life situation even today as we partake and join hands with another person. Relationships as you will see is not just a word. Its something real and very important. Without relationships there wouldn't be marriages or boy friends and girl friend relationships. There wouldn't be relationships.

We would just be individuals. That's not a good thing. That would defeat the purpose of life that we know, love, and respect. According to Dan and I quote, a simple definition of conflict might be the following: Conflict is the tension that results from incompatible values, desires, or needs. First, he said we must realize that conflict is inevitable in every relationship.

No two of us look at everything the same way. One doesn't need a spouse to experience conflict, however, in fact, many conflicts are internal, waged against ourselves for example, when we must choose between foods proper for our diet plan and those which we find appetizing but which aren't necessarily good for us.

Conflict isn't a bad sign in a relationship. Actually, the presence of conflict shows that the parties are involved with each other. In the long run, indifference is more likely to destroy intimacy. Confrontation is the road to trust and greater intimacy, provided that an air of love and respect can be maintained.

Yelling, name calling, avoiding the issue, arguing multiple issues, dredging up the past, blaming, assassinating another's character, interrupting, changing subject, and giving our spouse the silent treatment are all effective ways to tear down one another and destroy trust.

This isn't to say that couples can't fight, especially when the air must be cleared. Many people think the popular marriage encounter movement or being encountered means continual billing and cooling like star struck lover. That's unrealistic. In a marriage we must relearn how to fight, so that we fight fairly. A fair fight involves deciding what the core issue is, sticking to that issue, exploring and working to resolve it while avoiding the pitfalls of name calling.

It means fighting for your relationship, instead of fighting to win. A couple experiencing conflicts must decide together what is the most central issue of conflict for them; then formulate a question around the issue. The attitude I have about any issue determines my behavior. The first step is to gain awareness of my own part in the conflict.

Once I open myself and look at my part in our conflicts, I find it easier to move to the last step of the options. Write down anything and everything that comes to mind to solve the conflict is similar to brainstorming. Lets talk about "love and Commitment", as expressed by Frank Vilaasa, according to him, one of the qualities of love is benevolence.

A genuine love brings with it a spontaneous wish to do whatever we can for the well being of the person we love. Why is it so difficult to give that person a second chance? If you sincerely love that person it shouldn't be a difficult decision to make. What Frank Villassa is saying makes a lot of senses because what does you have to loose? Nothing.

If the relationship is important, and the person is important in your life, you'll do everything possible to save that relationship. He says in our heart we feel that we will always be there for them if they ever need us. This he said is an akin to a commitment. But it is a commitment that is freely given. Love of this kind only flourishes in a climate of non-possessiveness, in which freedom of each other is fully respected. True love he said on both sides, is primarily concerned with the happiness of the beloved. Our own welfare is secondary to this. A lover does not consider his or her personal agenda. Their concern is for the other person, unquote.

He said and I quote, If love is missing from our lives, it is not necessarily a sign that something has gone wrong, often, it is a part of our soul's purpose to experience the absence of love. It is said that you don't know what you've got till its gone and this is certainly true about love. It is he said, my belief, and the essence of most spiritual teachings, that our spiritual purpose as human beings is to evolve into consciousness.

Nowadays, he said and I quote, the woman's personal agenda has changed. She still wants security, but mostly she can take care of her own financial needs. She is getting more interested in sex for its own sake, rather than as a bargaining chip. Men, nowadays, he said, still wants sex. They continue to enjoy a financial advantage over women. They don't feel the same need for security that women feel. Men wants freedom, but they also need love and intimacy.

However, they are afraid to express this need. Firstly. because being men. they are afraid to express any sort of need or vulnerability. And secondly, because they fear that if they do express this need, their partner will ask for a commitment from them.

So men used sex as a way of snatching some sort of emotional nurturing for themselves, and remain very guarded about what is happening in their hearts. He said and I quote, when a commitment is finally agreed to, then the actual love that is experienced in the relationship usually starts to decline. The main reason for this is that the commitment came from the head rather than from the heart, unquote. In view of what has been said couples who handles their differences and conflicts poorly, put downs, hostilities, and harsh views of one another are most likely to develop serious problems within their relationship and marriages. The problem will dictate what you will do and say. And are a lot of emotions and feelings involved when there is a problem. Be careful with emotions. Emotions can help you and also destroy you and your relationship and marriage. It can cause you to do and say the wrong thing, and its usually out of anger, frustration, disappointment, pain, and of course the problem itself. Remember, feelings are things that is happening within you. Your thoughts, good or bad. Emotions are feeling, feelings and emotions will determine what you do and don't do. Lets talk about love of affection and surely we all have problems showing and expressing our love of affection to our partner at some point. Don't sit there and say no. I never did.

Some where we refused to do something because of whatever reason. According to this article from the internet, and I quote, we all have our personal feelings about how much physical affection we're comfortable with. For example, people who've not experienced much physical affection like me and others, much positive physically affection when they were growing up can be shy and self—conscious about showing love in this way when they're adults, but this doesn't necessarily mean they're cold or uncaring.

Regardless of why he feels this way it's something the two of you will need to find a way to move past, or else the problems in your relationship becoming more severe. A person can't changed the way they behave unless they're made aware a change is needed so you so you should talk to your partner. Its likely to require compromise on both your parts. When a partner feels dissatisfied and unhappy in a relationship but one carries on quietly, resentment can builds over time until one day explode, making things break down in a much more traumatic, unquote.

No one can tell you what to say but sometime to say "I'm sorry" will be all you need to say. But again, not in all cases. I don't know what happened between us. Where did we go wrong.

I honestly the God love you. Please don't leave me. I don't wants to loose you and what we have together. Please stay. Please give us another chance. I'm not perfect and therefore admits my mistakes. Its not to late to save what we have and that's each other.

These problems and we all have them are the root, and concerns of our relationship, believe it or not, and its painful to say, but their the caused of broken relationships between friends. families, and especially in marriages.

And you know its not what you say that hurts, and most times destroys a relationship, and marriages, it's the words being spoken, the words coming out of your mouth in a thoughtless way. and without feelings, causing that person to feel empty and less like a human being.

Its almost like a train is about to derail because you said the wrong things. you spoked the wrong words, and causing that person pain and to feel like shit. You know when that happens fire from the dragon mouth reaches out and tries to burn the living hell out of you. Why be bitter in times like these? It doesn't make senses. Be nice and be polite and be respectful of each other. Because when a person is hurting the other person is also hurting and in pain.

Why? Because your fighting and wanting the same thing and that is each other. Sometime a kind word is all you need."Because words are powerful". Sometime the unspoken word is the word that can hurt you. When there is a conflict of interest or a misunderstanding, love weakens, and it therefore becomes fragile, and when that happens, look out because all hell is about to break loose. When that happens you don't want to be anywhere near or in that disaster area. Because you will definitely feel the affect of disappointment, anger, frustration, and intents aggressive strength over powering the control of the individual.

Because they are at the brutal stage of the relationship as things heats up. This is the most dangerous stage of the relationship as it causes you to act irrationally, psychologically, and physically out of control. At this stage of the relationship you don't care what happens as in O.J;

although he was proven not guilty. So what really happened? The glove didn't fit.

According to this article by Write, Unknown, and I quote. One of the most important skills that anyone can learn in life is how to manage his own emotions. So much of how life will go for a person depends on how well she can do this. Without being able to control how she handles negative emotions, a person will go through life reacting with anger, sadness, and hostility depending on the whim of the events in her life.

Psychologists call what we're discussing here negative affect regulation. The two most important skills in marriage are to be able to regulate your own negative emotions when you are upset and to be able to regulate your negative emotion when your partner is upset. We believe there are some ways that husbands tend to have a harder time regulating their own negative emotions when their wives are upset. Many husbands acts out their wife's anger is the problem. That really isn't so. Unless she's expressing her anger in a hostile and invalidating way, it's neither wrong nor uncommon for one mate to feel angry toward the other from time to time.

Husbands, the most powerful thing you can usually do to help your wife calm down when angry is to really pay attention to what she's saying. If you are serious about doing everything you can on your end of the relationship to make it all it can be, here are some simple guidelines you might keep in mind: Do positive things for your partner and the relationship. Most people know what to do to please their partner. Do you regularly do the things that make a difference?

Decide to let negative or annoying comments bounce off you. If there are ongoing concerns you need to deal with, deal with them at a time when you are both calm and you can get your partner's attention in a constructive way. Be the best person you can in your relationship. Take responsibility for your own issues, personal growth, and awareness, and mental and physical health. Many people put all kinds of effort into personal improvements when they're "out on the market." Yes, this is a crass way to say it, but it's the truth.

We've seen it and you've seen it. Why not give that kind of effort to taking good care of yourself now? If more people did this, fewer people would end up looking for the next relationship. In the face of problems or pain in relationship, too often people think."I married the wrong person!" Thinking this way leads to depression and hopelessness. A great marriage is predicted not so much by your finding the right partner as by your being the right partner, unquote.

Insults and put downs. What are the harmful affect of insults and put downs? It can trigger a wrongful reaction. It can caused you to do and say the wrong thing. It can caused a violent and destruction. It can caused anger and arguments which can lead to violent, verbal and physical abuse. It can lead to broken relationships and marriages, and separation of families.

It can lead to domestic abuse and force to spend time in jail facing all kind of charges maybe even prison. It can lead to divorces, and finally death of a love one, and sometime the entire family. It can lead to mental anguish. Stress, and psychologically uncontrollable behavior.

Avoiding these problems. Peacefully, calmly, and maturely talk out your problems. Don't use insults and put downs as a weapon. Remember a sharp tongue can cut deeply and penetrate your soul causing all kind of problems to surface.

If you feel that your not getting anywhere seek professional help. Whatever you do if you value that relationship don't give up on each other. Don't play the blame game. Don't point fingers at each other. Don't accuse the other. Take responsibility for your actions. Once its spoken you can't take it back. Its called opened mouth insert foot. Saying I'm sorry, sometime is not enough. A sharp tongue can hurt and sometime kill. That's why you should be careful, very careful what you say. It can cause a reverse reaction.

What does that tell you? If you know and what a person don't like especially women "don't do it". Because its only going to piss her off more and furthermore make the situation worse. Does that make senses or is it clear as mud? The purpose of "what if" questions and general questions in nature should help you avoid major conflicts in your relationship and marriage. Secondly, they should help mode your relationship and your marriage as you grow in unity making it better.

When a relationship problem strike and surface the first thing we asked is "why". Again, if you know what a person don't like especially a woman" don't do it. Because when it strikes its too late. You then should be asking not why, but what can we do to fix the problem? You owed it to your relationship, to the person, to do the right thing. Don't stand there star gaging like noting happened. Men, women expect you to step up to the plate and be the man even if their wrong. Maybe it wouldn't hurt if you was to slap yourself in the face a couple of times.

Can you imagine the reaction you would get from her? Women are like apples because as time passes they ripen and get sweeter. That sweetness and tenderness men is very important in any relationship.

When you do have a problem especially the men try to remember the song "Rain Drop Come Dropping On My Head", and asked yourself, what does that song means to me, right now, this very moment. Would you be surprise to know how that song can intervene and probably help your relationship? Its not the song that's important.

It's the words and what those words means to her. A song men can sometime soften a problem and strength a relationship. Maybe even save your marriage and your relationship. After all that is what we're talking about. Music is what makes the world go round. The world is you. We are the world. Women likes to be told men I love you even doing the worse of times especially doing the worse of times.

Take her into your arms and look deeply into her soul through her beautiful eyes of pearls. Kiss her gently and never to let her go. Shower her with your love of affection. Massage her body of soul and admire her beauty as you stroke her freshly long and beautiful hair.

Do something dammit and kinder the night. Do what you need to do to save that relationship and your marriage even if it means sleeping on the floor next to the bed. No one sleeps on the couch anymore not even the devil himself. He surrounds you with his evil spirit of foolishness trying desperately to control you and your relationship making you kneel down to him.

Hopefully these questions and understanding of situations will save at least one relationship if not more.

When things happens we tend to say and use the following expressions. such as how dare you, how could you? I'm not pretty enough for you, you don't love me anymore, why did you do it, are you that hard up for sex, is she better than me, how long has this been going on, I though you love me, how long has this been going on, what made you do it, what about me, what about us, that explains the phone calls, all this time you have been cheating on me and I thought that you were working, the calls in the middle of the night, doing meal time, it was her wasn't it, you have another what. Who is she? Your what "Gay", and the list goes on an on. These expressions are important to know and understand.

Because in almost every relationship doing conflicts of misunderstandings, and turbulence times in our life between man and woman these expressions are used. They are used in a very ugly and harsh way to express dislike, anger, and frustration. Its normal for men and women to be upset when these things happened."The expression is, open mouth insert foot".

Because in times like these when your angry, you will say anything without thinking, and usually the first thing that comes to your mouth. You don't necessary has to mean it. The reason and key word is "hurting", or hurt if you will. According to the dictionary, hurting. And I quote. means to feel to cause to feel pain. Mental suffering. Anguish. A wrong or harm. Suffering, and I quote, physical or mental pain or distress, unquote.

What happens when the other person is in pain and suffering from what has taking place? You need to understand that it was something unexpected. If you love that person by all means your going to hurt, and be put in a state of shock. Most time your not going to know how to react or how to respond. You may simply scream or start crying. You might start throwing things. It all depends on what's going on at the moment. Its not something that you take for granted. Its almost like your heart is coming out and the feeling of being stabbed in the back. It affects everyone differently. You might not react to it until hours later. Because the shock might be too overwhelming. Now, and when you do all hell will break loose and sometime with a destructed force. You will feel like the walls are closing in on you.

You will start asking yourself questions. What did I do? What if anything I did to cause this? Your head will feel like a rock and headaches will set in."There will be no peace". Its not something that goes away overnight. It will take time, weeks, and maybe even months or longer. You will feel like going crazy. Because the problem might be too much for you to deal with. Shock can kill you.

Pain is torture. Hate is as strong as love. Do you ever wonder about the strange car parked outside or the phone ringing in the middle of the night? Suddenly a click and a call back? An unusual body odor or smell?

I'll get it. Redness on the side of the neck? Someone at your door, a woman if you will, wearing dark glasses, and the list goes on and on.

Surely you get the picture. Are you should that nothing is happening? These are red flag warnings telling you most times something is going on. Most times a person knows when something is not right. That is the perfect time to confront the person.

By confronting the person you're confronting the problem. To do nothing is wrong. You'll have yourself to blame. And. you may not like the way it ends. Anything is possible."Stump it out now". Slam your foot on the brakes and say, enough is enough. Respect those red flags of warnings. Your relationship and marriage may depend on it. If that person and your relationship means anything to you, you will take action or die trying. Don't let nothing come between you. your relationship, and your marriage. Lets talk about jealousy in Relationships, by Advice Diva, and I quote. Everyone has been on both sides of the fence.

Most of us have experienced a jealous lover and many of us have been in a relationship where we curiously find ourselves being insecure and jealous by nature. Without going too far into the psychology of jealousy, you should understand that jealousy is not an innate feeling that we are all born with; rather it is a learned response that people have developed over time to deal with certain situations.

We have and I quote, the ability to feel anguish and emotional sorrow, and jealousy is one way we cope with these feelings. Jealousy can real its ugly green head at any time. You never know what will set it off. Some people can be completely at ease with one lover and insanely jealous with another lover. Jealousy should not be confused as a sign of love. Severe jealousy is the exact opposite of love.

When people exhibit jealous rages, they are only destroying the relationship they are trying to save. People use jealousy as a legitimate weapon of defense to protect what is rightfully theirs.

Jealousy attempts to prevent the annihilation of love, but it only helps it along. Experiencing these jealous rages will also further lower the your self respect because it causes you to stoop to the lowest of acts. It destroys more than just the relationship.

Jealousy is invariably are to maliciously hurt the other person. The best thing you can do is recognize that your jealousy may be unfounded and then open the line of communication, instead of brooding on thoughts of infidelity, simply tell your love how you are feeling as soon as you start feeling that way. To help get rid of jealous behavior you must leave all of your doors open. Meaning, you must not keep anything hidden or locked away for your love to get suspicious or distrusting over. You sometime wonder where to go from here within your relationship when things seen to have gotten out of control.

You wonder if the tasteful of your relationship has gone cold. Let us therefore talk about the ingredients of happy relationship by Lindisima, and I quote, according to her article, time is a very valuable asset. Time lost she said is never gained. If you will spend time wisely, you will never regret it. We are not in this world forever. So if you can do good today, do it.

The person may never be there tomorrow, even if you cried your eyes out at their grave; it won't bring them back. So use every opportunity you get, so that you will have memories stored up in you. Never get busy for the little things in life otherwise you will find them gone. Never take life for granted and learn to strike a balance. If you neglect your partner, they may become vulnerable to any man who would come along and give them the time that you don't. Be attentive when your partner is speaking. Watch their expressions and learn to know their gestures too so that you are able to read their actions easily. Know what angers them or makes them smile or laugh. Get involved in the little details of their lives too.

Yes, even knowing the type of lipstick she uses and the aftershave that he likes. Know the birth dates and anniversaries too. Know the little intimate details makes the relationship exciting an it gives both of you enormous joy in knowing about each other. For a solid foundation, trust must be established. Once trust is established you will begin to open up to each other. It takes a while to build trust but it only takes a second to destroy it. Be sincere to your partner and tell the truth.

If you have kids, tell it; been married before, say it; you have a health problem, mention it.

Avoid hiding things that may or will eventually come out and cause an explosion and destroy the relationship for good. When your partner trusts you with a secret that they have never told anyone else, then do not ever use it to manipulate them or use it as a weapon to inflict pain on them the day you have a fight. Be careful what you say especially the promises that you make.

We are tried and judge by our words. For a relationship to grow it needs to be nurtured. Understand the strength and weakness and build on them. If your personalities don't match and you are not satisfied, please walk out ASAP before any serious involvement happens. When the relationship is not worth pursuing, it is always wise to end it in a polite way.

Give it a thought before you do, just in case there is still hope to save it. The important thing is not to make enemies but to walk away feeling free and having a clear conscience knowing that you made the right decision. Be able to live with that decision and ensure it's the right one. If not, you may realize too late that you made a big mistake. In other cases it's a simple and straightforward thing to do like when you find your partner in bed with another person or when you have an abusive relationship. There is someone out there for you and it's not the end of the world, unquote.

Things That A Woman Don't Like

A woman don't like being ignore. She don't like being without money. She don't like being lied to or cheated on. She don't being yelled at or taking advantage of. She don't like being treated like trash. (do this. do that). She don't like being force or push into making decisions or wrongfully and blindly pressure. She don't like to be rush or told what to do. She don't like a sexual cold hearted man (someone who does it only when he wants it) having no regard for her. She don't like it when you don't know what she likes. She don't like it when you don't understand her. She don't like being control, bully, or intimidated. She don't like being verbally or physically abuse by no man. She don't like being put in an uncomfortable position. She don't like it when a man don't defend her honor, (letting others disrespect her or walk over her), or when you say nothing. When you do nothing. A woman don't like it when she's getting the shitty end of the stick. (It could be anything).

She don't like her feelings hurt or being made a fool of. She don't like it when you turn your back on her. She don't like it when you don't answer or takes too long to answer the phone.

She don't like it when she has to force you to love her. She don't like it when you cheats on her.

She don't like it when you spikes her. She don't like it when you stresses her out.

She don't like it when you force her to do the wrong things and refuses to look at her. She don't like it when you can't hold your liquor. She don't like it when you can't control your mood swings and your anger. She don't like it when you pays no attention to her. She don't like it when you ignore her feelings.

She don't like it when you don't show appreciation or a simple thank you. She don't like it when your not passion toward her, touching her, hugging her, holding her hands, and of course kissing her. You must be able to do those things (Passion is important). She don't like it when your silence, not willing to communicate with her.

She don't like it when you don't respond to conversations, questions and answers. She don't like it when you don't take her anywhere. She don't like it when you don't prepare a meal sometime. She don't like it when you cause her to feel lonely and isolated from your family and especially from you her man. her lover, her everything. She don't like it when you take your anger out on her. She don't like it when you accuse her of doing something or blaming her for the cause of a love one dying. She don't like it when you ignore her birthday giving her nothing, when you ignore mother's day giving her nothing.

She don't like it when you expects her to do everything. She don't like it when you ignore her sickness, pain, and suffering. She don't like it when you cannot support her financially.

She don't like it when you can't show tender loving care for her. She don't like it when you can't say her name. She don't like it when you can't say "I love you".

She don't like being kept waiting or wakening up late for work. She don't like being late for work and having to rush. She don't like not having something to wear. She don't like it when she's treated like a second class citizen or unimportant.

Things That A Man Don't Like

Men don't being force to sleep on the couch when there is a problem. Men don't being put in a position of having to beg for sex. When a woman embarrasses him in the present of his friends.

When a woman has an affair with someone else. When a woman

complains too much about money. When she complains "simply" too much. When she tries to make him out to be the bad guy. Being blame when something happened.

A man hate it when a woman say. get out of my bed you asshole. When she say either you leave or I'll leave. When she say get the fokken out of my house. When she say don't put your dirty hands on me. When a woman say, you're a fokken asshole, how dare you do this to me. Just because you are a woman it doesn't make it right. When a woman say shut the hell up. "You bastard". When a woman say, this relationship is over. A man don't like it when a woman uses sex against him. (to denied him the pleasure of sex). When a woman uses sex to gain a position. When a woman uses sex to get a promotion. When she throws something out of anger into your face. When a woman slaps you in public. Insults you and puts you down in public. A man don't like being blame for everything.

A man don't like being bitten. A man don't like being repeatedly asked the same questions over and over again. A man don't like being hit by you or by objects because your angry. A man don't like to be slap or falsely accused or taken advantage of by a woman man don't like to be threatened by violent (because your angry). A man don't like it when you loose self control when your angry. A man don't like it when you ignore his feelings. A man don't like it when you over hear a conversation of another person say "she's my ex—wife, you turns and looks at him, and say "your next". A man don't like it when you uses his words against him or takes what he say wrongly. A man don't like it when you accuses him of lying. Lets talk about the "D" word. a word that deeply affects relationships and of course marriages. It is the end of what was. of what uses to be as an important part of your life.

Beyond the scope that its not an easy decision to make either of them. But its sometime necessary to save whatever part of you is hurting. and of course for the sake of children. and for their health and welfare. Therefore lets take a look at an article by Paul Mauchline. and I quote. In recent years, newspapers and magazine articles, books, and television shows have focused on the subject, are you the one for me? This question is one of the most common topics of discussion among friends and family.

We would all have to agree that committing ourselves to a

relationship, and eventually to marriage or a common law relationship. is probably one of the biggest decisions that, yes, this is the one for me, and makes such a commitment. Divorce according to him is necessary in cases of physical or mental abuse, or in the of two people who are so incompatible that they never should have been together in the first place.

I have heard he said, many excuses for why relationships fail: he/she has changed since we met; we just grew apart; the love just disappeared from the relationship; we weren't compatible; financial troubles got in the way; we weren't communicating anymore; he/she was unfaithful and cheated on me.

Why are we failing, today, he said, in recognizing what we want as individuals, and what we want and need from our relationships? Why are we at least half of us selecting the wrong partners. I do not feel he said that we are honestly examining the question, are you the one for me. As much as we may think we are.

Relationships are a big part of life for most of us. It is part of our human existence that we choose a mate, share love and intimacy, provide comfort and security for one another, and in many cases, have and nurture children together. Sometimes, though, we fool ourselves in the initial euphoria of love; we are not honest with ourselves about the things that bothers us about our partner. We hope that these things simply will go away. We might ignore upsetting issues and allow them to pass without challenging them, or avoid topics of discussion that could lead to disagreements. We might be hesitant about asking questions of our partner that may reveal potential problems for our relationship.

Why do we insist on having a relationship when we know deep down inside that this person is not the one. Why do we choose to set ourselves up for emotional hurt. There are many answers for these questions, but fear is probably the greatest motivating factor for these choices.

We fear being unable to find" Mr Right", someone with whom to share our life. We fear living alone. We fear being the last of our friends to be in a committed relationship. We fear the financial hardship of doing it alone in a society of two—income households. And. of course we fear growing old and dying alone.

In other issues and concerns he said, in an ideal world, the man or woman with whom you choose to spend your life would be adored by your family just as quickly as you initially fell in love. Family outings, holidays and celebrations would feel as though your partner had always been a part of the family and you would never feel the need to choose between them.

Let your family he said, get to know your partner in multiple situations, and make sure they have some one-on-one time to chat. It might be difficult at first, particularly if your family is being childish about it. But this might be the only way to let your family see how wonderful your partner is. We need to make compromises he said in relationships, but we should not sacrifice our personal dreams and goals for them. By ignoring potential problems, we abandon ourselves for the sake of the relationship, unquote.

In any relationship especially in marriages money is a concern and if your thinking about getting married. So therefore lets take a look at this word no matter how wonderful it sounds, it could cause you problems in months and years to come. We will be enlighten by articles by various writers on this such as they are identified later. Maybe money or the burden of a financial problem doesn't affect your relationship or marriage but others do.

Financial problems according to Komal K. and I quote, can affect your marriage if you let it.

As long as your partner knows to be responsible with spending, then you'll have to cut corners and do without certain things. But yes, sometimes finances and stress of not having enough money to pay bills can sometimes affect the way you treat one another.

But don't let it, if you need to sit down and budget every single penny so that your partner can stay home and raise the kids then do it. Yes most financial problems may affect your relationship with your partner, or your kids since it causes a lot of stress, sometimes even resentment by the bread winner, unquote.

Symptoms of financial problems by Crown Financial Ministries, and I quote. Without question, family problems seem to increase dramatically during economic slumps. Ignoring God's Word. Usually families with financial problems only recognize the symptoms of the problems (such as unpaid bills) or the consequences of the symptoms

(such as repossession of property). They seldom identify the real underlying causes of the problem.

Most of the symptoms of financial problems face in today's society—business failures. Foreclosures, bankruptcies, out of control debts, two-job—families, and divorce-can be traced to a central problem of ignoring God's financial principles as recorded in His Word. God's financial principles and instructions are not complicated or hard to understand. They were designed to free His people from financial burdens and not to blind them with an unattainable set of dos and don'ts."Now it shall be. if you will diligently obey the Lord your God, being careful to do all His commandments which I command you today, the Lord your God will set you high above all the nations of the earth".

Unfortunately, though, since the mid—1950s God's principles have increasingly been ignored by families who have adopted a get-rich-quick mentality by using easily obtainable credit to purchase "what I want, when I want it". Now, a generation later, we are reaping the burden of sown seeds of moderate debt in the form of overwhelming excessive debt.

Once the credit cards have reached their maximum limits and other sources of readily available credit begins to tighten, financial pressure begins to build. Finally, in desperation, a bill consolidation loan is obtained. Usually within less than a year the credit card debts return, making the end result worse than the beginning.

At this stage many Christian families try to pacify the financial pressure by buying something new or going on a "get away from it all" vacation. However, these usually have to be financed with credit, so again the end is worse than the beginning. When financial pressure reaches the boiling point, with no apparent way out, either the couple take it out on one another—resulting in divorce—or they file for protection under the bankruptcy law in order to start over again. However, if God's principles were not learned during the process, the same financial problems will be present in the second or third marriage or after the discharge of bankruptcy. Although symptoms of financial problems can be devastating, it is much easier for families to practice prevention rather than recuperation. As such, there are four basic preventive measures that families can exercise to counterbalance unbiblical financial practices to prevent the symptoms of financial problems such as, abstain from borrowing, saving, making hasty decisions, develop a budget, and conclusion, lived by sound biblical financial principles, unquote. Money problems by Nayda l Torrres and Vervil Mitchellm, and I quote. Money is not dollar and cents, its is also a symbol of personal attitudes toward life.

In a marriage, the first essential step is to a acquire financial attitudes that will harmonize with what you and your spouse want out of life. As a rule, happily married people are successful not because they have no problems, but because they have learned how to face problems and arrive at working solutions.

You may not realize that quite a few money problems can stem from your emotions. Solving money difficulties, not resulting from low income, requires both rational planning and insight. Many families do not talk about money management until they have problems. An already shaky relationship can get worse under the impact of money problems and heavy debts.

Soon after marriage, a couple may incur big debts because of too many purchases or commitments. Then they might be face with a medical emergency. a cut in pay or unemployment. Up until the emergency occurred. The problem may not have been serious.

However, as creditors press for payments and the budget tightens, quarrels begins.

Your attitude about money are influenced by your environment and your past experiences. Good family relationships and economic security are greatly dependent upon values and attitudes toward money. Family need to develop and understand their attitudes toward money, and decide what true personal or material value means to them, and then they need to clearly define their goals for economic security. Goal setting is one of the first steps in a financial management program. Goals provides incentives for good management. One reason many people fail financially is because they have no long-term goals for which to strive. As a result, their lives and their income are frittered away, unquote.

How to solve money problems by Michael Pollick and I quote. Many relationships experts rank financial issues second only to infidelity as a root cause of martial strife or dissolution.

Indeed, how a couple handles money problems can be a real-time litmus test of their line of communication. Few people enjoy discussing their finances either out of a fear of failure or an overly-developed sense of pride. This is why some married couples find themselves living far beyond their means. The solution to almost every money problem is more money.

This may sound oversimplified, but many couples lose perspective when caught up in a heated argument over bills. If an unexpected expense arises or a routine bill suddenly balloons, some couples may start to play the blame game. It was the other person's negligence that created this expense, or it was the other person's wasteful habits that caused the spike.

It is important for spouses to realize the difference between one's family and in-laws. One family may be comfortable with loaning money to relatives, while the other may feel it's not a good policy. It's important to discuss both viewpoints on family loans and reach a compromise before the need arises. Many arguments between partners over money problems actually have little to do with the issues at hand.

A number of people have deep-seated emotional issues where money is concerned, and those issues often come out during arguments. Both spouse need to realize that financial success is only one small element of their martial relationship, unquote.

What If. Why and Have You Questions

Why does a woman spend hours shopping?

What if a woman tells you that you shouldn't be married?

Why does it take a woman longer to dress?

Have you ever wonder "Why" a man don't understand a woman?

Why do they spend hours in the bathroom?

What if the love is gone and there is no sex in your relationship or in your marriage?

Why does a woman fix her plate last?

Have you ever wonder "Why" we say the things we do?

Why does a woman complains about the simple's thing?

Have you ever wonder "Why" what make a man get upset?

What if a woman tells you I will find someone who will treat me better?

Why does a woman cry so much?

Have you ever wonder "Why" some men don't cry?

Why does a woman throw your clothes out the door, window, out of the closer when she feel or have suspicion that you are cheating?

Why are men just the opposite?

What if no matter what you do or say you can't satisfied her?

Why does she feels that you don't pay enough attention to her?

Have you ever wonder Why" some men have problems expressing themselves?

Why does a woman go out of her way to please a man?

What if a woman yells at you for no reason because she can't find something?

Have you ever wonder why, when there is a relationship problem, the woman is usually the first to say something, to speak out, and to confront the problem. Why is that so important to a woman?

Have you ever wonder how a woman knows when your lying and not being totally truthful?

What is a woman tells you if you really love me you will let me go?

Have you ever wonder "Why" some men cheat?

Have you ever wonder how a woman knows when your not feeling well?

What if a woman say. I was better off without you. I should have never married you?

Have you ever wonder why a woman likes her privacy?

Have you ever wonder "Why" some men feel afraid and nervous around women?

Have you ever wonder why she gives you strong looks?

What if you want sex and she's not in the mood?

Have you ever wonder why a woman stares deeply into your face?

Have you ever wonder "Why" some men don't talk much?

Have you ever wonder why a woman feels that she can have her way with you?

What if a woman tells you that you don't know what love is?

What if a woman tells you I can't take this anymore?

Have you ever wonder why just being with a woman will make everything alright?

Have you ever wonder why a woman worries most times more then you?

Have you ever wonder why a woman will trash a place when she's angry?

Have you ever wonder why a woman gets upset for no reason?

What if a woman tells you that you never did anything for her?

Have you ever wonder why. when a woman find out that your cheating, that she will go to great length to find out who that person is?

What if a woman continuously compares you to her other marriages and relationships "putting your down. and making you feel like your nobody."?

Is it true that a woman is more emotional when she's hurting (as in anger) than a man?

Why does a man calls a woman a bitch?

Have you ever wonder "Why" some men treat you like an animal in bed?

What if she simply refuses or stops cooking?

Why does a woman calls a man "you bastard"?

What if she accuses you for the relationship breaking up?

Why is sex so important to some women and not to others?

Have you ever wonder "Why" what makes a man a man. What make him do the things he do. and say the things he say?

Why when you say something women uses it against you?

What if a woman is pregnant by you, doesn't tell you anything, goes away for awhile, comes back, and later plays a song over, and over again, telling you that she don't love you anymore?

What about "stop the car syndrome"? Can't you just hear those brakes squeaks? Saying, don't do it. Damn I told you don't do it. I told you don't it. Why didn't you listen? Like you had a say on the matter. Don't you just like it when your brakes talks back to you?

Why does a woman feels that she must leave when things don't go her way?

Have you ever wonder "Why" some men are violent, and have problems controlling their temper in a relationship?

What if a woman says I married the wrong person?

Why does a woman feel that when something happen we should apologizes first or at least say something?

How do we deal with these problems. These are relationship problems that men and women faces everyday of our lives?

The what if problems in a relationship and also in a marriage are problems that we don't talk about. And the reason is simple "they can be misunderstood, they can be taken the wrong way, they can hurt and therefore cause pain and suffering, and henceforth destroy a marriage and a relationship. We tend to close our eyes to these types of problems.

We don't want anyone to know. Afraid of loosen that person. How does these problems affects a marriage and a relationship. What are we to do. According to Frank Vilaasa, when we feel discontent with our lives, we often misinterpret this feeling. We think our dis—satisfaction comes from the fact that our outer circumstances are not as good as they could be. If we could just get a better job, a bigger house and so on, then satisfaction will be ours. If out pointing a finger at anyone although it takes two to tangle, and hold true in a relationship and in a marriage. But it is true that women are first to blame the man in most giving situation.

Knowing that, we, us, men should not take what they say or do out of content or misinterpret what their trying to tell us. We, us, men, can sometime misread the message that a woman is attempting to transmit to us. We sometime takes it the wrong way and that's when attitudes and problems set in. and lead us to believe other things.

Its amazing how our mind can control us. Maybe that's what they mean when they said a mind is a terrible thing to waist. The situation and words being expressed can sometime caused us to think negative and act it out in our mind. The situation has a lot to do with what we do in life. Whatever you do, don't do and say the wrong thing.

Don't let the situation and words being used control you. You control the situation. Men you must understand that a sharp knife of a woman's tongue can cut through the thicker skin causing pain and torture all at the same time. Their just being what they are, a woman. Men, you must understand that a woman will speak her mind and say what she feels at the moment. Yes it will hurt. It's a lesson learned. Hopefully it will cause you to think.

Some men say I understand my woman. What a foolish thought. You'll never be able to understand a woman. Do they want us to understand them? No, they want us simply put and that is to be a man. Women don't always mean what they say. Its their way of expressing their feelings and emotions. And it's a good thing. According to this article by a Writer, name unknown, and I quote, you should set aside time to practice uninterrupted. Thirty minutes or so should be sufficient to get started with using the sequence on some of the problems you want to solve. Look he said over your problem inventories together. Construct a list of those problem areas as so indicated above, what and what if, in which each rated the problem as being less or serious. These are the problem areas we want you to use to practice the model at the start.

We want you to practice with very specific problems and look for very specific solutions in the model. We recommend that you set aside time to practice the problem discussion and problem solution sequence several times a week for a couple of weeks. If you put in this time, you'll gain skill and confidence in handling problem areas together, unquote.

The Write, also state that, and I quote, hidden issues reflect the unexpressed expectations, needs, and feelings that, if not attended to, can cause great damage to your marriage. The main theme of hidden issues relates to the extent to which you feel loved and cared for by your partner.

Such issues are often triggered when people feel that their partner isn't meeting important emotional needs, unquote. The articles are by SaSuave.com, hope they will be of help for you within your relationship and your marriage. The true intention is to help you, show you the important of relationships and how to solve the simplest problem that invades your life and well being each and everyday as you live.

Because they will be problems and mistakes will be made as you live and live together with each other. Hopefully living together will brock out the lack of attention that a woman need from you, the man in her life, and the man in the woman's life.

As you read these articles think about what it means to you and to your relationship and marriage, and how you feel in regard to the information provide. Because it is provided to help us all as we grow in relationships, to give us guidance, to give us strength, and hopefully love and understanding, and how to deal with unforeseen problems within our marriage and relationships and there are many, and there will be many more as they approach us with or without warning. Your Mind is More Important Than Your Mouth, by Craig Reeves, and I quote. For some reason, we tend to focus a lot of attention on what it is we SAY, instead of HOW we say it. Think about it... What's really the most important aspect?

Remember back when you were young, and you might have done something wrong to your parents. If you were a good kid, you would say something like " Im sorry," mom" or something along those lines. If, however, you said that exact same sentence in a tone that showed a little too much attitude, they'd say something like "Watch your tone, boy!" or something like that. Do you get what I'm saying. It doesn't matter what you say nearly as much as HOW you say it. If you walk up to a woman and you say."Hey, what's up? With 3 different attitudes, you are going to get 3 different responses. Just like when you were young. and you said " Im sorry mon." in 3 different ways, you would have gotten 3 different responses. We all know that confidence is very important when approaching a female.

If you are not confident, the woman will notice it, and will naturally be turned off by it. I.

Craig Reeves, mentioned earlier that WHAT you say isn't nearly as important as HOW you say it. If you walk up to an attractive woman and say, "Hi there, how's it going? In a manner that displayed a LACK of confidence, this alone would turn her off.

Scary, Huh? What can you do if you really ARE nervous and unsure of yourself. Its how you look at the situation. It's your mindset. It's your belief. The only surefire way that you are going to be able to correctly approach a woman is if you adopt the correct mindset and attitude of doing it. What you need to do is to speak and act toward her as if SHE's interested in YOU as well. Your comfort level when talking to a woman will increase greatly if you start thinking this way, because you will no longer feel as if all of the pressure is on you, nor will you be trying to fight so hard for something (her interest) that you already have, unquote.

The Difference Between Feeling an Attraction and Feeling a Commitment, by David

DeAngelo, and I quote. I he said. Yes. I think that long-term relationships are wonderful, healthy, and can be a great source of joy and happiness. Amen."I've had many of them myself, and have enjoyed some great times as a result.

But here's the distinction: If you don't learn how to make a woman feel ATTRACTED to you at the very beginning, then you are taking a HUGE risk. Namely, that you're going to invest all of your time, effort, energy, emotions, gifts, money, and life pursuing someone who may or may not ever feel the same way about you.

If, on the other hand, you master the art of making women feel that GUT LEVEL ATTRACTION using only your personality, then you won't be GAMBLING as much when it comes to women and relationships. I think he said, that long-term relationships are great.

I just don't like he said the idea of investing a lot of time, energy, and money if I have no idea whether a girl even likes me ! How much better it is to know how to make a woman feel that excitement, tension, and attraction at the very beginning. This way you're not out of control, wondering where you stand.

Then, if you decide that this is someone that you'd like to spend more time with in the future, you can start doing more traditional "relationship" things (if YOU choose). A relationship based on two people enjoying each other's company and personalities is FAR stronger, in my opinion, than one based on gifts, money and favors. Take a moment right now, and think about the difference between ATTRACTION and COMMITMENT. Thin about the things that make you feel ATTRACTED to a woman, and then think about the things that makes you feel

ATTRACTED to a woman, and then think about the things that make you feel COMMITTED to a woman, unquote. The 7 Signs a Woman Wants to Be Approached, by Ron Louis & David Copeland, and I quote. 1. Saying "hi" right away. If you said "hi" to that woman at the coffee shop when you first saw her. and she didn't say "hi" back, you'd have a good idea that she's not very receptive to our approaching her.

If she did say "hi" back, then you both have a little invested in the relationship, and it will be easier to talk to her more later. 2. Assessing her "vibe". With some women, you really might get the sense that there is a wall around them that they are really in their own world. In that situation, the average guy will make this mistake —he'll assume that if he was better with women, he'd be able to break down that wall, talk to that woman, and get her into bed in 20 minutes or less. The truth is, some women are highly unreceptive, and it doesn't have anything to do with you, and there's nothing you are going to be able to do about it.

Stop idealizing her as "the perfect woman, who got away" an stop beating yourself up about it. 3. Check out her level of eye contact. If you are around anyone, you are likely to make accidental eye contact, unless that person is making an effort to make sure that eye contact does not occur. If you can't catch her eye, it doesn't mean that the game is over, but it might mean that she's less open to you than you might like. 4. Being a source of certainty that the interaction is going okay. Remember, most of the time, a woman is looking to you to gauge whether or not she should be tense in an interaction. If you seem relaxed, she'll be much more likely to relax, too. Providing that certainty is, much more important than having the "perfect line". You can bumble all over the place. but if you are a source of certainty, then you will have a much better chance with her. 5. See how she responds to comments, You can find if a woman is receptive by making some little comment, and seeing how she responds to it.

See how she responds, if she grunts or says nothing, she's probably feeling unapproachable. If she gives you an entire sentence, you are on your way. 6. Try a simple conversation—starter. Get this. it is permissible to start a conversation with a very tepid, non romantic question.

Look for something in the environment you can comment on. or something about her person that you can ask a question about. Then make your comment or ask your question. It's perfectly fine to start a conversation with."Excuse me. I notice some you have an Apple Laptop. How do you like it?

I couldn't help noticing your unusual necklace. I can't recall ever seeing one like that before. If you wouldn't mind me asking, what's the story behind that?" 7. Don't beat yourself up for "missed" opportunities. Sometimes you'll "miss" opportunities with women. Don't beat yourself up about it. We believe that this is true:"Missing", opportunities, and not beating yourself up about them, is part of learning to actually take opportunities.

Anger & Relationships—What You Need to Know, by Allen Thompson, and I quote. People get angry when they feel they have been treated UNFAIRLY. If a person feels he has been treated unfairly he will get angry. If he feels he has been treated fairly, he won't. It's as simple as that. The important thing here is not what happens to the person, but his "feeling" or "perception" that he has been treated a certain way. Whether he has, in fact, been treated unfairly or not is irrelevant. As long as he thinks he has been treated unfairly he'll get angry regardless of the situation, the outcome, or what happens to him. The Ten Most Dangerous Mistakes YOU Probably Make with Women.... And What to Do About It, by David DeAngelo, and I quote. 1. Being Too Much of a "Nice Guy". Have you ever noticed that the really attractive women never seem to be attracted to "nice" guys? But for some reason they were never romantically interested in YOU.

Women don't base their choices of men on how "nice" a guy is. They choose the men they do because they feel a powerful GUT LEVEL ATTRACTION for them. Being nice doesn't make a woman FEEL that powerful ATTRACTION. And being NICE doesn't make a woman CHOOSE you. Until you accept this FACT and begin to act on it, you'll NEVER have the success with women that you want. 2. Trying to "Convince Her to Like You. What do most guys do when they meet a woman that they REALLY like... but she's just not interested? Well. I have news for you... YOU WILL NEVER CHANGE HOW A WOMAN "FEELS" WHEN IT COMES TO ATTRACTION! You cannot CONVINCE a woman to feel differently about you with "logic and reasoning". If a woman doesn't feel it for you, how in the world do you expect to change that FEELING by being "reasonable" with her?

When a woman just isn't interested, we beg, plead, chase, and do our best to change her mind. 3. Looking to Her for Approval or Permission. In our desire to please women (which we mistakenly think will make them like us), us guys are always doing things to get a woman's approval or permission. Women are NEVER attracted to the types of men who kiss up to them..EVER. You will never succeed by looking for approval. Women actually get ANNOYED at men who seek their approval. 4. Trying to "Buy" Her Affection with Food and Gifts. How many times have you taken a woman out to a nice dinner, bought her gifts and flowers, and had her REJECT you for someone you who didn't treat her even HALF as well as you did?

Your intentions usually come across to women as over-compensation for insecurity. and weak attempts at manipulation. That's right. I said that women see this as MANIPULATION. 5. Sharing "How You Feel" Too Early in the Relationship with Her. Another huge unfortunate mistake that most men make with women is sharing how they feel too early on.

Most men don't realizes this, but attractive women are being approached in one way or another ALL THE. An attractive woman is often approached several times a DAY by men who are interested. This translate into dozen of times per week, and often HUNDREDS of times per month. Attractive women usually dated a lot of men. They have EXPERIENCE.

They know what to expect. You can't pull blinders over them. And one thing that turns an attractive women off and sends here running away faster than just about anything is a guy who starts saying "You know. I really, REALLY like you" after one or two dates.

This signals to the woman that you're just like all the other guys who fall for her too fast and can't control themselves. Don't do it. Lean back. Relax. 6. Not "Getting" How Attraction Works for Women. Women are VERY different from men when it comes to ATTRACTION. When a man sees a beautiful, young sexy woman, he INSTANTLY feel a sexual attraction. Do women feel sexual attraction to men based mostly on looks? Or is something else going on? Well, after studying this topic for over five full years now. I can tell you that women usually have their "attraction mechanisms" triggered by things OTHER than looks. Women are more attracted to certain qualities in men... and they're attracted to the way a man makes them FEEL than they are to looks alone. 7. Thinking That It Takes Money and Looks. One of the most common mistakes that guys make is giving up before they're even gotten started.... because they think that attractive women are only interested in men who have looks and money... or guys who are a certain height.... or guys who are a certain age.

But MOST women are far more interested in a man's personality than his wallet or his looks.

YOU DO NT have to "settle" for a woman just because you aren't rich, tall, or handsome. 8. Giving Away All of Your Power to Women. Earlier I mentioned that it's a mistake to look to a woman for approval or permission.

Well, another similar tactic that a lot of guys uses is GIVING AWAY THEIR POWER to women. Said differently, guys try to get women to like them by doing whatever the woman wants. Women are NEVER attracted to men that they can walk all over... Women aren't attracted to Wussies! 9. Not Knowing EXACTLY What to Do in Each Type of Situation with Women. Now I'm going to blow your mind... A woman ALWAYS knows what you're thinking. Women are approximately TEN TIMES better than men at reading body language. That's ten TIMES. And if you don't know exactly what to do and exactly HOW to kiss her, and you just sit there looking at her and getting nervous, she won't help! Approaching a woman, getting her number, asking her out, kissing her, getting physical... everything. It is VITALLY important that you know EXACTLY how to go from one step to the next with a woman... from the first meeting, all the way to the bedroom. 10. Not Getting HELP, This is the biggest mistake of all. This is the mistake that keeps most men from EVER having the kind of success with women that they truly want, These what and what if questions remind me of the story about Pam and Joel that was written by another Writer, I forget what his name was but hopefully you will enjoy read this story and learned from their mistakes.

The story and I quote. They had lost any creative aspect in their love making, tending to do the same over and over again. Those things worked, in that both were feeling relatively connected and both were usually having orgasms. But they'd come to a point where Pam's orgasms always followed intercourse, through Joel's stimulating her. Pam felt a bit limited in this, and Joel felt that they could never have intercourse and just relax right afterwards because he always needed to focus on helping her climax. And he did, and it was good that he did. Still, they felt there could be more. What Pam and Joel described suggested concerns other than specific sexual dysfunctions. For so many couples, if they feel something its not quite right or that something is limited about their physical relationship, one or both partners can too easily begin to wonder if there is something more at stake: Do they really love each other?

That kind of thinking makes a relatively common situation turn into a dangerous one. For Pam and Joel, the matter was really more about the development of bad habits wherein they had made their lovemaking a low priority. Unlike couples who simply don't have the time to devote to their physical intimacy. Pam and Joel had neglected this aspect of their relationship.

They decided they both wanted to increase their investment in physical intimacy. We developed a simple but powerful plan, called Your Plan for Romantic Success. Plans such as this one are highly likely to help couples move out of ruts, as long as both partners are committed and really follow through on what they've agreed to try to do differently.

This article suggest that you take the time to customize this list to suit your own tastes and priorities as a couple, and have as much fun as you can. Focus on being romantic and sensual (send flowers. romantic emails. whisper suggestive desires during dinner. touch his or her leg under the table. We know that talking as friends and sharing fun times are aphrodisiacs.

We hear this often from women but believe it's also true for men. Do not focus on orgasms or other outcomes. Pressure is not an aphrodisiac. Focus on wooing your partner, as opposed to taking his or her for granted. Men, be her knight in shining armor, and win her love and affection on a daily basis. Be sensitive to your partner's rhythms, needs and wishes, unquote.

This article spoked of winning her love and affection on a daily basis. I therefore would suggest that you know and understand what a woman likes. Here are a few things you may want to consider: Women like having their own spending money, of course their own checking account. They like it when the man takes charge of the bills making sure everything are paid without them having to worry about it. Eat out sometime (wine and dine them).

Close family and extended family relationship and spending time with friends. Being shower with flowers, and beautiful things, such as cards and kisses on their birthday, and special occasions. Being bathe and dressed by their man. (showing them tender loving care).

When their man sometime chooses their clothes for them. When their man opens the car door for them. When their man gives them a lot of hugs and kisses. (Sweeping them off their feet). When their man tells them how much beautiful they are and how loving she is.

When their man make them feel love, attracted, and important. When her man holds her hand and takes short walks. When her man takes her shopping and on trips together, the two of them. And most importantly when he treats her like a woman and takes care of her, loving her, and respecting her feelings and emotions. Relationships are too often taken for granted, and then the we sit back and wonder why.

If your relationship was important to you in the first place you would have secured it, safe guarded it, you would had protected it, and most importantly you would had held tightly to it never letting it slip through your hand. Who are the blame for broken and endless relationships and marriages? You are, we are not just that, everyone involved in that relationship is equally the blame, and equally at fault. Its time to let the rocks fall where they may. Women its time to stop blaming the man. Men it time to stop blaming the women. Its time to stop pointing fingers and take responsibility for your actions. Be man enough if you will and say yes I did it. Yes I wish that I could take it back. and yes your right. What ever happened to please forgive me. Baby I didn't mean to do it. I love you. Your everything to me. I didn't mean to hurt you. I never wanted us to end up this way. I didn't mean to say that.

I was afraid that you would leave me. That you would not believe me. I don't want to loose you. I'm sorry not just sorry but sorry for everything I put your through. Women, you know when your man is sincere. Men, the truth hurts sometime but we need to learn to swallow our pride. Men we need to stand up and be counted.

We need to stand strong and take the lead. Why? Because your woman expects you to and she has every right to do so. She depends on you. Respect her being a woman. Women respect him for being a man. The grass may not be greener on the other side. The old saying is there is a man for every woman.

But you should also remember there is a woman for every man. But do you want to go there? If not be smart and leave it alone. Is that really what you want? Why make two mistakes. Women, why choose someone over the man you have? Men, why choose other women over the woman you have. We need to think before we do. That word angry can cause us to do and say the wrong thing. Watch out. Be careful. Don't loose a good thing.

Everyday people are making these same mistakes when they could had been avoided. Conflicts people are something that we go through and experience everyday of our life. How we deal with those conflicts, issues, and concerns is what's important. If that man, woman, and that relationship means anything to you, you will do everything humanly possible to save to hold onto that marriage and that relationship. If you don't apparently you didn't care. But over the years you have planted the seed in the person head and heart that you do care, and that you love each other. What's up with that. Once the seed has been planted and begins to root in the person brain, heart, its hard and difficult to remove.

You have spider web and mold this person into your life this person feel and thinking that you'll be together for a long time maybe even forever like high school sweethearts.

So men take care of your woman and hold tightly to your marriage and relationship. Women are special. Women are precious and they deserves to be treated with love and respect, and above all like a woman. Women stand by your man and respect your man, and love him like no other.

Its time to take a serious look at marriages and relationships because time has changed and with time people have changed. Divorces are bad news. We don't need that. We need for families to stay together. Marriages and relationships are not like they were years ago. There was a purpose in mind, and that purpose was held dearly to the heart.

Because it had meaning. There was a value. There was love, trust, and devotion, and most importantly fewer divorces. Its not hard to understand why such a changed has compound over generation. There are many reasons and we uses them as excuses to do wrong.

Temptation, the devil made me do it. Are you telling me the devil controls you? If we want to compare generations years ago with our generation today what would you find? Were relationships long ago more unity and more strong? What about love, sex, and affection.

What did they do that we're not doing. Its enough probably to make you think? Its because marriages and relationships meant something in those days and it was real. Why is it that we don't place value on marriages and relationships? Is it hard to understand the relationship between a man and a woman? It takes two to form a relationship and two to have a marriage.

A relationship is not about one person. Because one person does not make a relationship. In a relationship you have a bond. a meaning of life between you. You have value and a purpose for being. something to work toward, something to achieve, and something to believe in. It don't come cheat. There is a price. That price is called trust. Because you must be able to trust that person. If you can't trust that person. You don't need that person.

As cold as it may sounded. But its true. Not being able to trust and depend on that person is like sleeping on a bed of nails. Because the trust in not there. Some people takes this for granted and when they do you can understand why certain things happens. I don't understand why we would let something so valuable and precious just slip through our fingers.

Something that we said we love and cherish forever. It makes you wonder as the expression is "when shit hits the fan". It makes you take notices that something is wrong. Something is not right. When you see that something is not right what are you going to do? Are you going to sit back and laugh? Are you going to put your head between your legs?

What are you going to do? And more importantly when? Naturally, the quicker you do something the better. If you value your marriage and your relationship you will. Why did you let it get that serious? Why didn't you do something when you saw the warning signs? Crying about it is not going to help. You should be kicking yourself in the ass, and asking yourself why you, didn't do something earlier? You should kick yourself in the ass. The damage has already been done. What more do you want? What more can you hope for? When you see something is wrong get off your ass and do something. Fight for your marriage and your relationship. Don't let it slip away. Fight for that special someone in your life. You'll be a fool if you don't. Fight for your marriage and your relationship.

If you can do that then you have accomplished something. There is no straight forward answers or solutions to a problem. This depends mostly on whose involved, family, friend, or relative. To fix such a problem should be handle with tender loving care, showing and giving respect to each other.

Respecting the problem. Respecting each other. Don't let the problem control you. You must control the problem. The seriousness of the problem can sometime overwhelm the situation and will determine how solvable the problem is. But it will take both of you and your willingness to do it. This is not the time to throw punches at each other.

That will only make things worse. This is not the time for insults. Sit down and try to solve the problem peacefully, if others are needed to accomplish this task of your indifference by all means involve them. It should be someone you both trust. Don't continuously argue and fight between yourself. It will only make the situation worse.

That can also lead to a broken relationship and in the case of marriage a divorce. In speaking of broken relationships, marriages, and the word divorce, what if something you did intentionally or unintentionally caused your spouse to feel betrayal, and she therefore accuse you of turning your back on her. What are you to do. Whatever you say don't let it be the wrong thing.

You will never hear the last of it. There will be no peace. It's better to start with I'm sorry. I didn't mean to hurt you. It wasn't intentional. It just happened. That is not always the right answer. Some women will accept it and some will not. Chances are, and men you know it's true, chances are a hand across the face will soon follow. (A right cross). Why is that? She is angry and stressed out. It's due to the problem and of course the angry and stress.

The anger has not taken control of here and the situation. The body needs to calm down. It could take days, weeks, and even months depending on the woman and the situation. The verbal and physical abuse will continue to happen, such as yelling, screaming, crying, hitting, bitting, throwing things, and insults and etc. A woman kindness toward you will become very bitter and ugly, causing the relationship to end but not always.

She will push you to a point of no return. She will use herself as a woman to physically take advantage of you. She may even threatened to get out of a moving vehicle. Women when mad, angry, and stressed out will do pretty much anything until they calms down. They called it being hurt. Their hurting and the pain of the hurting is too much physically and especially psychologically to bare. What about the man? Men also feel pain. (Not in the same way as women). But when a woman feels that a man has hurt her. She doesn't about how you feel.

It's how she feels at the moment. Whatever happens don't let her anger and stress cause you to do and say the wrong thing. Take control of the situation. Be the bigger person. Pick up the phone. and if necessary, call a friend, family member, and even your pastor, just call someone to help you through this crisis. If she wants out of the relationship, out of the marriage, let it end peacefully. In time the wounds will be no more. Wounds will begin to heal.

Don't beat yourself up. Don't be so quick to let your guards down. A woman is like a snake. She can come back at you again. Verbally an physically attack you when you least expect it. For example, what would you do if she over heard a man taking telling someone about his ex-wife. and turnabout and looks at you. and says" your next". What would you say?

What would you do? What if she tells a male friend in your present, that she would married him or someone like him. Wouldn't that be enough to make you vomit? So, please tell me what would you do or say? (Don't let your guard down). Thinking about it was clearly disrespect. disrespecting the person. Relationship, and the marriage. What does you do when there is no peace? Peace is so important at this time.

But when your angry and upset. How can there be peace? There is peace after the storm after everything has been resolved, your anger, your indifference, dislike, disagreements, and pain of torture has ease. You have just entered a world of the unknown the unwanted lives of sin. The dead will take over and control your thinking, your wisdom, your strength, using your weakness against you, and causing you to loose control of yourself. Emotions and feeling takes advantage of you. You are no longer in control of your senses. You are no longer in control of the problem or the situation. Your anger has taken over and now in control. The problem is not so important anymore. The anger is so powerful it has driven you forward to total destruction.

The pain is not important anymore. It's the situation that has driven you to that point of madness, anger, and the stress surrounding the problem making things worse. Stress can kill.

Stress can destroy you. Stress can cause you to say and do the unthinkable. Surely. we know what that is. When it happens. It hits hard. If you don't know how to control your emotions, feelings, and anger, conflicts, problems, and situation will control you, and cause you to do the wrong thing. Stay in control at all times.

No one wants a nasty divorce but it does happens. Than hate set in. walks through the door of hell although it my not be welcome, unwanted, and most times unnecessary. Why, why, why, why are we so prone to hate the other person, to hate each other. Don't you hate me bitch, don't you slap me. don't you yell at me, don't you touch me, get stepping bitch, why did you do it bitch, leave me the (F) alone bitch, get the (F) out of my bed. Get out now, and of course you son of a bitch. Step you fool. I'm leaving you.

Why are we prone to do and say these things. Stop letting the situation control you. Take control of the situation. Hiss more: You hadn't seen nothing yet. I can be as cold as you. I can cheat too, where are the suitcases, wait until I tell the pastor, you got some nerve, you asshole, don't mess with me. and finally, everybody thinks you're a nice guy, wait until they hear this.

You wait until they hear this you asshole. Anger, madness, and stress, believe it or not can caused all source of problems and more. Men, it takes a woman longer to get over anger and the hurt she's feeling emotionally inside. Do not use her words as a weapon or tool against her because she's hurting. She is telling you that the pain she feels is real.

She's letting you know how deeply she's hurting. When everything is said and done she'll apologize and show you love and there will be peace within once more. Men, do this please. I asked this of you. First of all take a look at the situation. Examine the problem, take a look at yourself, take a look at the other person, and ask yourself a question.

Where do we go from here. How should we deal with this problem? Can we discuss it together peacefully. Can I control myself. What are we to do? What if it does get out of control? Will she leave me? Should I just leave and not say anything? Should I assumed nothing has happened? Will it hurt my relationship? Will it hurt my marriage? Should we just kiss and make up? Men, there are times when we honestly don't know what to do.

We just wish it hadn't happened. Whatever you do or say. just remember your not the only one in pain. Your not the only one that's hurting. Children, if you have children they will suffer too. The pain and suffering will be just as deep, just as painful if not more. Problems no matter of the nature of it. The word travels fast and soon everybody knows and even the neighbors. Do not put your children in such an embarrassing position.

There will be so many questions asked of them by there friends and classmates. Don't let your children see or hear you argue. If possible end it quietly and peacefully. If of course you decide to get a divorce. Do it with a great deal of respect for yourself, and of course for the sake of the children. Do not tell your children until your both have the time to sit down peacefully and tell them together. Don't point the finger of blame at each other. That is not the time or the place. You'll be defeating the purpose of talking to your children. They don't need to hear that.

They don't need to see you arguing. Your children will have enough to deal with just knowing that the two of you will be no more. Don't make them hurt more than they has too. Although your no longer husband and wife, mother and father, under the same roof "Be There For Your Children". Assure them that they can visit and call you anytime, day or night.

They didn't caused your divorce. They are innocent just simply caught in the middle of what has happened between the two of you. They are not your problem. You are your problem. And it's between the two of you to solve it.

In conclusion, no one knows how their going to react to problems or situation until it happens. Lets talk about the "D" word. but remember it's not always the answer to your problem. It's more like running away from the problem because now as they say. "if its too hot get out of the kitchen". Well, problems cannot solve themselves and running away or trying to avoid them is not going to work either.

You need and you must stand strong and look each other into the face, into the eyes, and deal with it direct and with an open mind of intelligent but be forceful and respectful of each other opinion and respond to the questions. Do not attack each other respond but be open minded to the other person feelings.

Remember your not the only person that is hurting. Others involved are hurting as well and it could be many. Any way take a look at the following articles relating to marital crisis and situations, divorce, cheating, and ways hopeful to gain some control over your relationship and marriage problems as they presents themselves. Eppert Claims Over 90 percent Success Rate Saving Marriages. Breakthrough Method On What To Say To Stop A Crisis. by Dr. Lee Baucom, and I quote. Studies find that over 50 percent of married couples he said divorce.

The case is more dismal with remarriages, with some estimating 75 percent lead to divorce.

Half of all couple enter therapy to save their marriage and less than 20 percent report improvement from therapy. Understandably a couple in a marriage crisis are helpless, hopeless, and think divorce is the only alternative.

No marriage crisis appears overnight. Rather, the crisis slowly builds over time, with one person often caught completely off-guard, and the other claiming that he or she is tired of trying and trying. with no change. Dr. Baucom reports that the damage is done when one needs to have something change, but the other seems to be preserving exactly what the spouse wants to change. The other person, who wants the change, becomes more and more frustrated.

This he said leads to a pattern where a spouse suddenly announces that the marriage is over, and the other spouse is seemingly unaware that there is even a problem."I don't know he said how many times I have heard someone say" sure, it wasn't the best of relationships, but I didn't know that my partner was so miserable.

"Unfortunately. The "not knowing" is translated as" not caring" and gives proof that the marriage is over. More marriages die from neglect than anything else" theorizes Dr. Baucom. Often, it is a simple matter of life getting in the way. Strangely, something as important as marriage gets ignored. On our wedding days, no one expects their marriage to fail. And when people rate their priorities. their marital relationship always ranks in the top 4. But according to research, couples spend on average less than 4 minutes per day talking about issues that do not include schedules and the kids. As neglect sets in. the lack of attention eats away at the relationship, slowly eroding the capacity of the couple to form a substantial relationship.

At that point, it is only a matter of time before the issue arises that casts the marriage into a crisis. When it comes, one or the other feels the hopelessness of the situation, and moves to resolve the crisis by getting out of the marriage.

When the crisis is in full swing, he said. it sometime takes awhile for the other spouse to respond. Dr. Baucom uses this fact to create a path back to wholeness. He states that" too many programs treats the way back as one path.

But I believe there are 8 distinct paths that must be addressed differently. What is helpful at one stage can be destructive, or at least counterproductive, at another stage. The innocent beginnings of a crisis (neglect. lack of understanding. etc) can quickly spin into a crisis that puts the entire marriage at risk. At this point, the trajectory of the relationship can become unpredictable. But the path back is predictable, according to Dr. Baucom," How a marriage falls apart, that can happen in a million ways. But how a marriage recovers, there is only one path back".

Couples cannot simply get back to where they were when the marriage got in trouble. The marriage already had the beginnings of a crisis. Instead, it needs to get to a place where the marriage is insulated against any future crisis. In other words, an average marriage isn't enough in my mind. He said I want people to create an exceptional marriage!, unquote. The Trauma of Infidelity, by Dr. Reena Sommer, and I quote. There is no escaping it, finding out that your husband has cheated on you is not only shocking but incredibly painful. Even if your relationship has been admittedly troubled, it's still a devastating blow to discover that your spouse has been unfaithful to you.

No doubt. it's infuriating to find out that all the time you spent trying to make your relationship work.... it didn't mean a thing because your husband was involved with someone else. And perhaps you were wondering. "what is wrong?" or" could I be doing more? Perhaps you even blamed yourself for all of the relationship's failings.

If you were like most wives, you probably weren't able to bring yourself to consider that "maybe there was someone else! However, now that your are faced with the proof of an extramarital affair. you can no longer deny or ignore the painful truth that your husband has been unfaithful to you. Right now, you may feel that the only choice you have is between accepting things the way they are or ending it once and for all.

You are not alone in your feelings because there are thousands of wives just like you, whose relationships have been impacted by infidelity, who are in the exact same spot as you right now.

After all, it's hard to feel good about yourself when you've been dealt such a terrible blow.

It's difficult to make important decisions when you are emotionally distraught and unclear about what happened or what to do. Being bitter and angry is not a way to spend the rest of your life.

Nor is being distrustful, suspicious or jealous of anyone (especially other men) with whom you are involved. You deserve to move on and "The Anatomy of An Affair" will provide you with the tools to get your life back on track whether you choose to stay in your relationship or end it. Why women cheat. These infidelity statistics are pretty shocking! If you suspect that your wife or girlfriend may be cheating on you. or if you already know for sure that she's having an affair, then this could be the most important information you will ever read.

The Trauma of Infidelity, by Dr. Reena Sommer, and I quote. There is no escaping it, finding out that your wife or girlfriend has cheated on you is not only shocking but incredibly painful. Even if your relationship has been admittedly troubled, it's still a devastating blow to discover that your spouse has been unfaithful to you.

The challenge for any counselor or therapist is to help a couple develop a better understanding of themselves and each other as well as the circumstances that led to the crisis in their relationship. Once this is achieved, a couple is then in a much better position to explore options for themselves and their relationships.

Unfortunately, most couple who are faced with infidelity in their relationship rarely seek appropriate professional assistance. Instead they struggle on their own when they are most emotionally taxed and least able to cope effectively. This type of situation is similar to trying to put out a raging fire with a garden hose.

It just doesn't work, unquote. In conclusion, and I quote, according to Dr. Baucom. No marriage crisis appears overnight. Rather, the crisis slowly builds over time, with one person often caught completely off-guard and the other claiming that he or she is tired of trying and trying, with no change, unquote.

Personal and inner most feeling of others: by Sam Davidson, Love is like being in prison. You should imprison yourself hugging and kissing your partner and never to let her go. Prison teaches you to love yourself, others, and love for freedom. You should It should never be taken for granted and nor should your partner. I wish that I could take back many of the things I said that hurt so many people. It has been said "that love hurts" but insults cuts right through you. If I was given a chance at life to live my life over, I would have the greatest respect and love for my parent. Your parent are your first love and then the love of your partner whoever he or she may be. Those of you whose reading this story I want you to remember this.

The greatest love of all is life. Live it well and be good to each other. When its over it's over.

Love yourself love others, love yourself love your parent, love yourself love your family, love yourself love your father, love yourself love your mother, love yourself love your wife, love yourself love life, love yourself love freedom, love yourself love" God".

Love life to the fullest and religiously. Don't be like me. Life is too short. Love can be forever if you wants it. It's easy to say I wish I had. People take care of what you got. Love your partner always and unconditionally. Cling to your partner like there is no tomorrow. Worship your partner like you would the church or you might end up saying "I'm sorry.

A friend sent me this letter in confident hopefully you will learn how strange life can be reading the important events of her situation because it could happened to you, one never knows we only hope it don't. Out of respect for her, my friend, I will called her Jane. Jane writes Hi, Mr. Wallace, my husband and I have been married as you know for 8 years. Not once have he given me reasons to suspect him of cheating at least not until now.

We just the other week were talking about having a yard sale. I mentioned that would be a very good ideal. I was going through some clothes in the closet one day and felt something in one of his pants pockets. Ordinarily, I wouldn't take a second look. But I thought why would he have a number of another woman on back of a business card. At this time I'm thinking something is not right. Because he usually tells me about everything. A business card no doubt. I became for the first time in my life very suspicious.

Maybe it wasn't right but I had to know. I never thought that my husband would ever. ever. cheat on me. Mr. Wallace, please, am I wrong for thinking that way. Well, it will be hell to pay. No sleeping in my bed for the next few days. And damn sure no puss, no touching, and no kissing, for him until he has repent of his sin of adultery against me, his wife of many years.

The couch for him Mr. Wallace, the couch for him, I feel like choking his ass until he confess, I didn't want to accuse him or falsely accuse him of doing anything. But, you know how women are Mr. Wallace, your writing the story. So I purposely took the business card out of the pocket and laid it on the side of the bed where he sleeps.

Can you imagine what was going through my mind? I was like a bull ready to barbecue some beef. I was having a panic attack. My heart was beating fast so fast that I almost fainted. I thought we had a good marriage. After we have two children, Wrong! what could there be wrong? My husband if you was to see him always looks happy. Surely, sex wasn't the problem. Although it could be. Maybe, he's tired of having sex with me.

Well, you know as a woman that was the first thing I thought. How could he do this to me?

We have two beautiful twin girls. That crashed my whole day. My body was in shock. I felt like a stick that couldn't be move. I screamed and cried for at least an hour or more. Oh God then the phone ring. It was him calling. I said get your ass home now "you son of a bitch".

Mr. Wallace I'm sorry but I was really mad. He knew than that something was wrong. I have never acted like this before. But again, I never had a reason to. As he walked through the door I started hitting him and hitting him. I just couldn't stop. I was mad, angry, and deeply hurt.

He came toward me and I yelled don't you touch me. He had the nerve to asked me what's wrong. After seeing the business card Mr. Wallace, he didn't even deny it.

I slapped him I would say at least twice maybe three times across the face. I said you bastard you could have at least deny it. Not even to say I'm sorry. Mr. Wallace. he just stood there like ice looking at me. I said you will sleep on the couch for the next few days. He saw that I was hurting. He didn't even say a word just stood there like a damn stick. Not even a hug.

You know Mr. Wallace what kind of a man is that. Married for 8 years, Mr. Wallace, I had to write you, and its because of your story I didn't leave him. He have you to thank for that I know Mr. Wallace that your story once published will be a blessing to both men and women. I am a true believer that love is as strong as hate. How do you feel when a woman says I love you. You're my everything. You're the love of my life. I worship the ground you walk on. You are my world. I can't live without you. I can't sleep without you. My heart would simply hit bottom. My body would freeze and take notice of her beauty and understanding as she looks into my eyes. I wouldn't know what to say."Maybe not even what to do".

What drives a man to hate a woman, not just a woman but his partner, the love of his life? Don't blame it on the devil. The devil wasn't there. The devil didn't make you do it. I love my wife despite our ups and downs. No marriage is perfect. When we're having problems, ok, if love isn't the problem than what is it? Could it be over the years we have gotten too uses to each other? Some people blame their problem on money or the lack of it. We don't have a lot of money. not as much as we would like, but we're financially and personally better off than most. I think being together in a relationship, in a marriage for many years you begin to pull apart from each other, your marriage and of course your relationship begins to weaken when it should be the other way around. You wonders why this happens. Is it a test of faith?

Is it a test of your strength that you really love each other? Whatever it is just be there for each other, I appreciate my God given senses, the common sense he gave me to stand clear of problems and the strength to face them head on. I have a good woman. A good wife. She's my best friend and the mother of my children.

That means a lot to me. She dresses like a queen a queen I know she is, and takes care of me to the end. I wouldn't think of not loving such a woman for she is sweet to the core hanging on a tree looking out at me, at the star of David, as the rain drops so lightly upon her head Enriching the Seed of her Heart why pumping blood throughout her body, carrying the love of life, love of my life, to her brain above. For this I know she does with joy, loving me, hugging me, and kissing me.

She does it so well and with a smile. It's enough to make you wonder why we get out of bed.

This letter comes from a friend of my wife and I. and he writes. Brother Wallace, my man. I was talking to your wife the other night. She said you were at work. She told me about this story your writing. If you don't mind Brother Wallace, I would like to be part of it.

I have a lot to say especially about love. Love is only skin deep if you know what I mean. Years ago Brother Wallace people took love and marriage more serious. Today, well, it's not so. Their ready to break up with you, and divorce you in a second. And talking about money that's part of it, I'm just telling it like it is. Marriage isn't what it's cut out to be."Not anymore". Marriage is suppose to be between a man and a woman. That's not so anymore. The ring on your finger means nothing."Anymore". Am I lying? Look at the cheating going on between both male and females alike. Look at all the broken relationships and marriages.

Hey, someone needs to say something. Whatever happened to the words "I do"? You made a promise to each other. Broken promises. Broken ring. Broken marriage. Broken relationships. People today are getting married for the wrong reasons. Maybe its called "Free Sex". What your really doing is playing a deadly mind game.

You are putting yourself in arms way of a destructed force of unwanted trouble as it slides off the tracks heading for hell. And believe me it will be hell to pay. Broken marriages. Broken relationships. Broken homes. It will never be the same. Everybody suffers even the children.

My wife and I thank God everyday that we don't have that problem. But, I have seen too many marriages and too many relationships that does.

My wife Beaverly and I. Brother Wallace, have been married for nearly 16 years. Not once have I cheated on her or given her any reasons not to trust me. That's the secret of my marriage Brother Wallace, and this is the truth, she was my neighbor for many years. Because of that we got to know each other very well. It seen almost like we were dating.

Maybe that's why we're always there for each other. She is a fine woman and the love of my life. There is nothing that I wouldn't do for her. My wife Beaverly, Brother Wallace, is looking forward to meeting your wife. We'll have a great day of fun, fishing, and barbecuing. Anyway, love between two people Brother Wallace is a good thing. But the problem is it's so bitterly abuse. Brother Wallace, love is caring. Love is passion. Love is life. Love is taking care of family. Love is blind. Love is wakening up together. Love is action. Love is every lasting. Love is divine.

Love is knowing when to let go. Love is hope. Love is special. Love is great. Love is being there for each other. Love is never saying no. Love is watching out for each other. Love is strength. Love is a warm heart. Love is happiness. Love is trusting and believing in each other. Love is priceless. Love is sweet and deadly. Love is two hearts beating as one.

Love is what you make it. Love is never ending. Brother Wallace, you have the making of a good story. Surely, it will be a big seller, and men especially should buy it. It's like the last chance of understanding women. My wife Beaverly and I. Brother Wallace, we were talking the other day about things we don't think about and it's sex.

We were giving examples of what sex is. We have this kind of discussion from time to time among other things. We believe it helps to keep your marriage and your relationship strong, alive, and healthy. Sex, we said is good. Sex is great. Sex is gratification. Sex is communication. Sex is pleasure and pleasing. Sex is love between two people. Sex is never to say I'm sorry. Sex is emotional touching. Sex is alive. Sex is giving of ones self.

Sex is beautiful. Sex is wrapping arms around your partner. Sex is sweet. Sex is love.

Sex is reaching out. Sex is coming together. Brother Wallace again, thanks for receiving my letter and I hope to see it in your book. I will really make my day. This letter I'm very much impressed with and it was written by my heart to heart, loving wife Daphne, When relationships are not established correctly dreams can be shattered. Eighteen twenty, twenty five years ago later nothing is accomplished. Both are going into separate direction because no respect is given or received. It is not about you only. It's about the both of us. What we put in a relationship is what we reap. Commitment, honesty, and meeting each other needs. Forgiveness can also be the main factor in any marriage.

The husband responsibility is always be ready to defend and protect his wife in every and all circumstances. Women are created differently from men. Men are more stronger in voice and aggressive in voice and action. Men do not used your voice to manipulate and control your partner. Although woman can destroy, control, and manipulate a relationship she does it mostly with words.

Men should have the will power to either back off, run, or simply use kind words. In some cases woman just need attention. If men are not willing to use certain methods to keep a relationship using love, compassion, and understanding. Not mistreating the woman who gave birth to their children, prepared their meals, responding to their sexual desires, and all the good things a wife has to offer. Men should learn the method of comprising.

Even thought both sides should be accounted for their negative behavior. Women are more emotional and their needs should be taken into consideration. Many women are being physically and mentally abused and mistreated. They refused to seek help because children are involved. In some cases the wife or companion is unemployed.

Therefore she thinks that she can't survive on her own. Even thought the marriage is doomed.

Women continues to accept the pain and agony that is inflicted by the husband over and over again. Man please stop this madness. A woman is your equal not your slave. What home atmosphere would you like to establish? Who are women? What does a woman need from a man. Needs of women are : Love, emotional comfort. Needs to be told that I love you. Women needs to feel that your there for them and that they can depend on you. Value, worth, and dedication. God does not create junk! Our image should not be tarnished.

Men and woman finds different ways to control. If you treat your spouse disrespectfully they will disrespect you in return. In a marriage to make it better or worst we should not tear down the greatest gift which is love and respect. Connecting emotionally, physically, and spiritually will bloom into a meaningful relationship. Fight for your wife not with her.

Tolerance and love will conquer all. Sometime a woman can be seductive, and tricky. and the bottom line she just need someone to take care of her financially. Men needs to be aware that they can be tricked into marriage. If you think its too good to be true have someone do a back ground check before saying I do."The truth needs to be revealed".

The internet was the most popular technology that was invented. Men and women of all walks of life turns to the internet for love and sex. The lives of people are being shattered including marriages and serious relationships. It's very devastating when a pastor or priest are amen in high society is involved with an internet relationship.

The wives are humiliated and the shame is unbearable. There is also positive relationships coming from the internet, successful marriages for example, successful marriages, and long term relationships. When betrayal exist on the internet it could take you straight into the pit of hell. It can result even in murder. At times marriage counseling cannot help you, family is a no. no. and friends are even worst. How does one overcome and internet betrayal? If there is no sexual act get rid of the computer and asked the one being betrayal forgiveness. A number of these website especially those consisting of pornography can be very additive. If your heart and your conscience tells you that your additive to pornography you must seek professional help. Someone who specializes in that field.

To make a confession to your spouse not knowing how he or she will react without the presence of a professional such as a member of the clergy would be damaging to your marriage.

The internet can be the ideal place to find love but do not go over board because it can also destroy you. Finally, women we need to protect ourselves from the verbal and especially from the physical abuse by men. Women, try to talk and reason with your partner peacefully.

Do not scream or yell at each other. Reach out to each other. Caress each other. Hug and kiss each other although it may be hard and difficult. Women, screaming and yelling at each other can push you over the edge. It can caused all sources of problems, such as headaches, violent, hatred, heart attacks, and other medical emergency problems of that nature. Women, you don't won't that. Women, in order for that to happen and maintaining a sense of balance and self control doing disagreements and arguments, one of you must be the bigger person.

One of you must say "enough is enough". Women, once its over its over. Don't go back later, days or weeks later, and rehash the problem throwing it back into your partner's face.

Your marriage could end up in divorce and so can your relationship. Men be patient with your partner. And with the love of your life. She is your wife. She is your lover. She is your best friend. She is the food you eat. She is the pillow you sleep on. She is your everything.

Remember you were once deeply in love. Why throw it all away now? Men be the wall that can't be move. Be the last person to yell and scream."Better yet don't yell and scream partner". Look into her face and say Honey. I love you no matter what. It may seen sometime men that your woman wants a divorce, pushing you further and further apart.

But its not always the case. Even if she answered yes to your question of divorce and even agrees to a divorce. Its not always what she really wants. What she really wants is you. A Model Wife and Mother, according to the Bible, Proverbs : 31, 10,30, and I quote, Who can find a virtuous wife For her worth is far above rubies.

The heart of her husband safely trusts her; so he will have no lack of gain. She seeks wool and flax, and willingly works with her hands. She is like the merchant ships, she brings her food from afar. She also rises while it is yet night, and provides food for her household, and a portion for hr maidservants. She considers a field and buys it; from her profits she plants a vine yard. She girds herself with strength, and strengthens her arms.

She perceives that her merchandise is good, and her lamp does not go out by night. She stretches out her hands to the distaff, and her hand holds the spindle. She extends her hand to the poor, yes she reaches out her hands to the needy.

She is not afraid of snow for her household, for all her household is clothed with scarlet.

She makes tapestry for herself; her clothing is fine linen and purple. Her husband is known in the gate, when he sits among the elders of the land. She makes linen garments and sells them, and supplies sashes for the merchants.

Strength and honor are her clothing; she shall rejoice in time to come. She opens her mouth with wisdom, and on her tongue is the law of kindness. She watches over the ways of her household, and does not eat the bread of idleness. Her children rise up and call her blessed; her husband also, and he praises her:"Many daughters have done well, but you excel them all."

Charm is deceitful and beauty is passing, but a woman who fears the Lord, she shall be praised.

Give her of the fruit of hands, and let her own workers praise her in the gates, unquote.

Marriages and Divorce, Matthew, 19: 3-9, and I quote. The Pharisees also came to Him, testing Him, and saying to Him."Is it lawful for a man to divorce his wife for just any reason?"

And he answered and said to them."Have you not read that He who made them at the beginning 'made them male and female,' And said. 'For this reason a man shall leave his father and mother and be joined to his wife, and the two shell become one flesh'?"So then, they are no longer two but one flesh. Therefore what God has joined together, let not man separate."

They said to Him."Why then did Moses command to give a certificate of divorce, and to put her away.""He said to them."Moses, because of the hardness of your hearts, permitted you to divorce your wives, but from the beginning it was not so.

"And I say to you, whoever divorces his wife, except for sexual immorality, and marries another. commits adultery; and whoever marries her who is divorced commits adultery." His disciples said to Him."If such is the case of the man with his wife, it is better not to marry."

"But He said to them."All can not accept this saying, but only those to whom it has been given, unquote. Again, I hope your reading of this story will help strengthen your relationship and your marriage, and give you the knowledge and confident to move on with your life whatever happens. But if all possible try desperately, patiently, faithfully, and full heartedly to solve your problem in peace. Don't let thumbing blocks come between you, your relationship, and your marriage. These thumbing blocks could be anything even a person, or disagreements. It could even be money, bills. and burden of hardship involving others. Let talk about money and how important it is within a relationship because you cannot live and survive on love along. A person wouldn't think that money affects your relationship and your marriage. But it does and to a great extent causing all kind of problems. No matter how good or how strong a relationship or a marriage is money problems cause a relationship and a marriage to break up making you feel very small, mentally, and financially stress out. First of all you need to understand that money is important in all relationships especially in marriages. Second, women have needs and wants. You as a man must respect them. If not you will be eaten alive. There will be no peace. Do whatever necessary and right in the eyes of God keeping your woman happy saving your marriage and your relationship. Money problems can be hard and difficult, and once you fall into that hell fire its crawling on your knees to get out.

Men will discuss their problems with other men but not so much in detail like a woman. We're not so open and women hate that. They therefore see you as being soft and afraid to say or do anything. A woman on the other hand can only do so much to help you. They will digest and analyze the problem and later spit it out. But it is up to you to solve the problem. Don't keep her in the dark. Your relationship and marriage depends on it. Don't take that part of your relationship for granted. There is no relationship without money because you cannot live on love along. You cannot have fun, go anywhere, or do anything without money. How strong is love?

How strong is your love? Is it stronger than money? Have you heard the expression? Money talks and bullshit walks? Well, that is not the case here but it does make a different when it comes to relationships and marriages. Those of you who are in doubt and disbelief should think seriously before entering into a relationship. The stress and unwanted harassing phone calls believe it or not will haunt you driving your to madness. If your marriage and relationship means anything to you" yield to the warning signs. Don't let your relationship and marriage fall through the cracks pushing you further and further into the gates of hell. A woman don't want to be stress out over bills. It was once said that love conquers all. When you look at relationships especially broken relationships it makes you wonder. Why are so many people falling out of love and relationships? When you think about it and opens your eyes the reason is staring you in the face. It's almost like looking into a crystal ball. The woman begins to feel trap in a relationship and in a marriage going no where. The ship is sinking and you are on it.

She will ask you where do we go from here? What if anything can we do? Remember, its not what you do. Why is that so important. A woman likes to be taken care of by you "the man".

She likes to feel sexy and desirable. You as the man must take care of her financial needs wants, and desires. She will leave you sitting on your ass if you can't. A woman likes to be wine and dine. A woman should be free to spend her money, her pay check on things that she personally need and desires. She will love you for it. Your marriage and relationship will be bless. Sex cannot solve your money problems. Therefore do not look her in the eyes thinking it can. You will be painfully and unworldly disappointed. She will feel less like having sex if sex at all. Sex is not the solution."You are". Although some people are blindly mistaken thinking it is. It will come a time when you will feel threaten by the questions. You will feel helpless and a shame. No more. No more sex. You can look but don't touch. The bed is no longer a place of rest. It feels like a bed of nails. It is cold as ice. The spark is gone. The relationship is no more. The marriage is gone. There is nothing more to hope for. Or is there? Your woman looks over at the Jones. They don't appear to be having your problems. They are driving fine cars and people are there all the time. Cook out two to three times a month. They are dancing and having a good time. You on the other hand, "well" what can I say."No fun". Do you really think she's going to stay with you? Have you forgotten that a woman married you for?

"Better" not for worst? You can't say goodbye. She's gone. Many things can weaken and take control of a marriage and a relationship. Most importantly don't let it happen to you. We have this ideal that everything is alright. This has been a fairy tell for a very long time. It's now time to wake up. It's time to stop living in the past. Stop assuming that everything is alright. A woman will not hastate to tell you when something is wrong. You need to do something about it. A woman will say what's on her mind."That is a good thing". The brain is a terrible thing to waste. Well, so is love. a marriage, and a good relationship. If your woman is happy you'll get the sex. Surely, what has been said is important but how much has been understood? Don't let money come between you, your marriage, and your relationship. You only have each other.

When that happens it's the end of what was. Hate and hatred can set in destroying everything causing violent between the two of you. Once violent set in anything can happen ending your relationship and marriage and that means divorce. According to Miranda Marquit, and I quote.

1st Timothy 6.10, for the love of money is the root of all evil. Which while some coverted after they have erred from the faith and pierced themselves through with many sorrows"(King James Version). When we let money come between us an our spouse, we are indeed "moving" asunder". We know that when we marry as Christians, we were expected to try and make it work.. This piece, though, is not one that focus on the merits of divorce and Christian marriage in some cases. This is a look at how we can strive toward being one in marriage finances. Unquote.

According to Joe Beam, and I quote, if you have accepted God's truth about you and your past, you need to move to the next step: You need to let go of any spiritually or emotionally harmful feelings and have for those in your past. You'll never be set free from your past—no matter what God does for you—if you choose either to (1) hold a death grip on the hateful feelings you have for those who hurt you or (2) cherish intoxicating emotions you felt for those with whom you sinned. God offers a new present as He continually points you to a wonderful future. but all sinful emotions you hold in your heart act like superglue to cement you to the evils of your past—either the evils you've done or the evil that were done to you. For both types of continued harmful emotions—as drastically different as they are—the solution is the same. Whether it's love or hate, passion or bitterness, fondness or revenge, you can only find peace in the present if you let go of the past an look to building an intimate future. You can't let go harmful emotions if you can't forgive. Anyone who holds hatred, rage, bitterness, anger, or desire for revenge must forgive and "forget" if he or she even wants to be truly free from the past.

Any intense in our life can be summoned by willing it to memory (unless. or course. it was so distressing that the mind refuses to catalog it in memory in an event-specific amnesia)."Forget the former things; do not dwell on the past". Letting go of harmful emotions does not only apply to people who hold on to hatred but also to people who holds on to love or passion for someone other than their spouses. We as family dynamics sometimes work with people who have had affairs and have asked for reconciliation with that partners. We remind these couples that they have many things to work out and do our best to give them a good "jump start" on their healing through one of our eight-week marriage courses.. Most of the time we see great spiritual and marital growth as we watch God work in marvelous ways in the renewed relationship. If you find yourself dreaming, fantasizing, or belonging for a lover, you must accept the fact—both intellectually and emotionally—that the relationship was sinful and distasteful to God. He made it abundantly clear that He thinks of sexual sin, sin outside the confines of marriage. The acts of the sinful nature are obvious: sexual immorality, impurity and debauchery; idolatry and witchcraft; hatred, discord, jealousy, fits of rage, selfish ambition, dissensions, factions and envy; drunkenness, orgies, and the like, I warn you, as I did before, that those who live like this will not inherit the kingdom of God.. If you continue to romanticize any sinful relationship you've had—either before or during your marriage—you give the memories of that relationship the power they need to keep you from growing in love and intimacy with your spouse. If you want to make your marriage all that it should be, you must recast your thinking about any adulteries, homosexual encounters, sex before marriage, or any other sexual activity which does not meet the strict standard of God, unquote. Whatever you do, have respect for yourself, your spouse, and of course for the relationship and the marriage.

My name is Alvin Wallace, age 58, born on the 27th day of February 1952, in Douglas Georgia. I am married to Daphne, and we have loving children both boys and girls. We live in Oklahoma City. I take pride in believing that the moon is the center of life as it changes from size to sizes shaking my life to what it is today. My mind is centered around growths as I leave the State Of Georgia from which I was born while my wings crosses over into the State Of Ohio being driven by my aunt and uncle. This enhanced my well being into the schools of that state graduating years later from South High School. As the earth spins on its axie I found myself jointing the Army in which I served for 16 years, and later transitioned into civilian life working as an emergency medical technician. That bouned me into the world of writing and the discovery of my writing ability in the year 1997 and 1998, such stories as 0000-an airplane story, U.S. MARSHAL, WOMAN OF LEATHER, AND THE SEA WARRIOR. This was when I truly discovered the fulfillment of writing and the joy it has given me over the years. I was inspired to write through the divine devotion that I have a gift, and a turn of the wheeel to express myslef, and my enthusiasm through what I love best. Writing has the ability and the magnitude to take you places you have never been before.